POLLY IN MY POCKET

Cautionary Tales Of Camper Van Life

Oliver Gray

Sarsen Press

Published by Sarsen Press

Copyright: Oliver Gray, 2020.

Cover design and layout by Richard Williams

Cover photo by Birgit Gray

Contact Oliver Gray at www.olivergray.com

ISBN: 978-1-5272-5568-5

Printed and bound by CPI Group (UK) Ltd, Croydon, CR0 4YY

1

HELLO POLLY

What do you do when you become a pensioner? Obviously, you buy a caravan. Or, in our case, a camper van.

It had always been a dream and, back in 1980, we thought we'd achieved it. We bought a sweet little split-screen VW camper from a New Zealander who'd been travelling round Europe. The cheap price should have alerted us, and of course it was an immediate disaster. It was all kitted out in wood on the inside, like a gypsy caravan, but that made it very heavy and the engine was buggered. We only went out in it twice, once to Reading Festival and once to the New Forest, and on both occasions we ended up being towed home at vast expense.

Eventually, I took it to a garage in King's Worthy, where I was assured by the two dodgy brothers who owned it that they would be able to repair it. They kept it there for weeks, getting me to pay them intermittent instalments to buy the necessary parts, before finally pronouncing that it was in fact irreparable and would have to be scrapped. That needed paying for too. A few weeks later, I was walking in Winchester and our lovely van drove past in perfect fettle, driven by one of the brothers. I'm still angry about it today.

People like me won't admit to being "retired". It would be tantamount to conceding that useful life is over. Besides, I have to continue to do freelance bits and pieces on account of a pension deficit. But the unpalatable truth was that our publishing business was no longer viable and had ground to a halt, so technically I wasn't in full time employment any more. Birgit, on the other hand, positively revelled in taking early retirement, after many years of dedicated service in the NHS. She was now committed to having a good time and getting on with doing a load of travelling while her much older husband (me) wasn't too decrepit. She also received a small legacy when her mother passed away, so it was logical that the camper van option would crop up again.

One day in 2016, we were on our way back from visiting friends in Devon and were passing the Somerset Motorhome

Centre near Taunton. We'd often driven past it before and thought about stopping, but never got round to it. This time was different. "Let's just have a quick look for a laugh," I said. Within an hour, we were walking out having bought a camper van.

For such a cautious couple, this was unprecedented. But we both just fell madly in love with "Polly Pocket", the sweetest little van in the universe. She's absolutely tiny, but suits my womb complex to a tee, because she's so unbelievably cosy. Despite her unambitious proportions, she has everything. She's got heating, a "kitchen area" with gas stove, a grill, hot water, a sink and of course a fridge with room for loads of beer. She even has a small loo and a cleverly designed wardrobe. I've always considered it slightly patronising that people call cars and boats "she", but Polly is plainly feminine in nature, so "she" it is. We adore her.

The first trips were to festivals, a cunning way (in my mind) to justify going to even more festivals than before. The feeling of overwhelming smugness as you climb into your comfy warm bed as the storm rages outside and everyone else is getting drenched in their miserable tents is ... well, I bet we are hated. Another early outing was to the caravan site at Eype, near West Bay, where the wind and rain were so strong that tents were literally being blown into the sea and Polly was rocking around like a boat on a storm-tossed ocean. But were we bothered? Of course not. We simply snuggled down with a little DVD player and some box sets and watched them for hours, occasionally boiling a kettle and dunking biscuits in hot tea.

The plan to drive round Europe was daunting for many reasons. Firstly, we'd be away from home for a long time. Secondly, my motorway driving phobia would mean that Birgit would have to do the bulk of the driving. And thirdly, largely unspoken but always there as a worry, was the issue that we'd be cooped up together for a long time with no escape. I'd read numerous articles about people's marriages foundering after retirement, as they discovered that spending all their time together in close proximity exposed all their flaws and annoying habits, leading to arguments and upset. And that was just on account of being in a house together. In deciding to spend six weeks in a camper van, we were taking it to an extreme that could have been a challenge.

I can tell you that it was all fine. "Give and take" is all you need, and doing lots of stuff so you don't get bored.

For Year Four, we decided to take the advice of countless friends and head for Sicily. The day of departure was our thirty-eighth wedding anniversary, May 12th. The plan was to leave later (and thus return later) than in previous years, following the notion that the weather should be more summery. We thus were primarily on the lookout for campsites with swimming pools, as, in the weeks leading up to departure, we pored over the green ACSI books which are the twin bibles of anyone looking for out-of-season campsites in Europe.

The principle behind these books is quite simple, the practical reality of them slightly less so. Campsites have to try and gain as many customers as they can in order to be able to survive out of season. There's a certain level of staffing and infrastructure that makes it impractical for many of them to shut down completely when there aren't many holidaymakers around, so most of them remain open all year, catering for the odd nomads and drifters who pass by, but mainly for people like us: wizened pensioners who've spent their "lump sums" on a caravan or camper. We are the people who not only can, but actually want to travel out of season. Not being restricted any longer by school holidays, we have the freedom to travel when we want. And we don't want to travel in high summer when the campsites are crammed with families with noisy kids. We love kids, by the way (and lord knows, we've paid our dues in this respect for a couple of decades), we just want peace and quiet when we go on holiday.

The ACSI idea is to tell campsites that they will provide them with out-of-season travellers, who are attracted by the lower prices they will pay if they produce an ACSI card. It's normally only a couple of euros cheaper than the standard price, but who can resist a bargain? You do, at least, know that on an ACSI site you will find water (more of that later), electricity (more of that later) and showers and loos (more of them later). Many campers like to pull up by the side of the road and just sleep anywhere, but we decided quite early on that that wasn't for us. It's a bit scary and you are more reliant on everything in the van working as it should, which isn't always the case.

The ACSI books aren't that easy to navigate. There are actually three of them. The system is based on two main ones, roughly the size of small telephone directories, plus a small one in the form of a 150-page booklet. The small book contains maps of all the countries in Europe divided into small portions. Scattered around these maps are small blue blobs containing numbers. These blobs indicate campsites. The idea is that you seek out the area that you want to stay in and have a look at the various campsites before deciding which one to choose. This is the simple part. Having decided on the number, it's now time to look in the actual camping book, which contains detailed descriptions of each campsite.

There's a photo which makes each one look impossibly idyllic, a brief description and very vague instructions about how to find it, plus a tiny map that is of very little assistance.

The difficult bit starts with the section that tells you what facilities the campsite does and doesn't have. The information is presented in the form of letters, but to understand what the letters mean, you have to go to six separate keys. In numerical order, these keys are as follows:

1. Regulations
2. Location, ground and shade
3. Sports and play
4. Water and recreation with shops and restaurants
5. Washing up, laundry and cooking and toilet facilities
6. Miscellaneous

Within each of these categories are letters indicating what facilities are available and what rules there are. For example, **1f** states that only one dog is permitted in low season when on a lead, **2d** indicates that the site is located by a lake or recreational pond of maximum 0.1 kilometres, **3q** indicates that crazy golf is available but it also has an asterisk telling you that crazy golf is not included in the price, **4d** tells you that there is an indoor swimming pool with a sliding roof, **5h** reassures customers that there is a senior citizens' shower with extra wall supports and **6n** tells you that there are shopping opportunities in the vicinity (up to 10 km away). Each number encompasses up to 24 letters, in fact you get the feeling that they only stopped when they got to z and didn't have anywhere else to go.

You can see that it isn't practical just to open the book and have a quick look to see whether the site is suitable. In fact, you need time, patience, excellent eyesight, a degree in advanced algebra and highly acute brain power to make any sense of it whatsoever. This is why we always make a point of leaving a lot of time to examine the evidence on the various campsites in advance before making a decision. Even that doesn't guarantee that you haven't overlooked something or misread the letters.

By way of illustration, here is a randomly-chosen entry for a campsite in Holland:

1. ABCDEIJKLMOPQ
2. ADGIJKLPTVWXY
3. BKLMNQRUVWZ
4. (B+G 30/4 – 15/9) JP (Q+S+T+U+V+Y+Z)
5. **AB**EFGIJKLMNO**PQRST**UVWXYZ
6. ACEGJM (N 0,3km) QRTV

Some of the letters are printed in bold but to this day

I haven't worked out what the significance of that is. I've already lost the will to live before I've reached the end of line 1.

For us, the only really important items are: whether there is an electrical hookup, whether there is a restaurant, whether there is a shop, whether there is a pool and whether there are any washing machines, but the variables between the possibilities encompassed are quite substantial. For example, do you pay extra for the electrical hook up? Is the swimming pool open all year? Is it indoor or outdoor? Is it heated? Does the shop sell fresh fruit? Do the washing machines take coins or tokens and, if so, how many? Much of this information can be worked out by delving even further into the microscopic hieroglyphics of the ACSI book, but in general it's normally better just to ask at reception when you get there.

Polly Pocket had been "Winterised" (yes, I'm well up with all the technical terminology). In practical terms, that means that, when there is a threat of frost, it's crucial to drain the water from everywhere in the vehicle, because, were it to freeze, it could potentially damage various components of the van. We discovered this in year 1, when I hadn't heard of the concept of Winterisation and just left the water in. Water in the van is in three separate areas, namely the water tank (containing the water you plan to use), the waste tank (containing the water you already have used, referred to rather unpleasantly as Grey Water) and the hot water tank, which is a boiler. It was leaving water in this last one that caused the original problem.

When I came to switch on in the Spring, the water simply came spouting out of the bottom of the van. A friendly neighbour worked out that the water filter, a tiny, flimsy plastic device, had simply cracked in the frost and needed to be replaced. Luckily, the local caravan shop stocks just about every spare part imaginable. When I took in what I thought must be a relatively obscure item and asked if they had one, the reply was, "Of course sir, this happens all the time". That should have been reassuring, but actually, it was rather worrying, as, being a complete dunce with anything practical or technical, I was beginning to see that there was more to this lark than simply driving around and sleeping. Polly Pocket, despite being minuscule and twelve years old, had actually been quite expensive, the reason (and attraction) being the range of features included in her make up, actually suited to far bigger and posher vans. For that, read "things that can go wrong". Little did we know that this was the tiny tip of a large iceberg.

Now I'm going to try and explain some of the other

complexities involved in little Polly. Aside from the three water tanks, there's a heating system. How lovely and cosy! But the heating is very odd. How would you expect such a vehicle to be heated? By gas, maybe, or electricity? Polly Pocket is heated by diesel. Don't ask me how. You just press a button and, after a moment, without the engine being even switched on, hot air begins to emerge. It's very efficient, but I don't trust it. If diesel is so polluting that it's already banned in city centres and soon to be banned outright, what the hell are we breathing in and what is it doing to us? There is definitely a faint odour to it, like you smell at petrol stations. If I wasn't already worrying enough about the potential emissions from the gas system, this was a danger too far, except possibly in the most extreme stages of hypothermia while wild camping. So what we've done is buy one of those little tiny heaters that people use on boats, that look like a Star Wars lance and emit just enough warmth to take the chill off. But that can only be used when plugged in on a camp site.

So ... electricity next. As with any other vehicle, there is a battery under the bonnet that is used to start the engine. It's not strictly relevant to anything that goes on in the van, apart from if you want to charge your phone when not plugged in. Any time you are plugged in to an electricity supply on a campsite, you don't need to worry about anything electrical. There's a plug socket in the van that you can use for an electric kettle, a hairdryer or a DVD player, and the lights are all powered from the connection, which takes place through a long cable which is stored in a little cupboard towards the back of Polly. There is also something else called a "leisure battery", which is concealed under the seats. This battery provides power for lights while the van is not plugged in. Apparently (we've never dared try it out) it can last for up to three days or more, but it doesn't provide you with power for any of the above-mentioned appliances.

The third source of power is gas. In the equivalent little cupboard on the other side of Polly are two gas canisters, rather like those you use with a gas barbecue. They are attached to a rubber pipe which disappears up into the body of the van and powers the cooker. That means that, even if you are in the middle of nowhere, you can boil a kettle or warm up some baked beans. But the gas cooker is the only means you have to do any cooking. There is no equivalent electrical device, so if you have no gas, you either have to eat cold food or go out to a restaurant. It's therefore essential to make sure that you always have a good supply of gas.

The fridge is even more horrifically complicated, in that it is hybrid (or even tribrid, if such a word exists). It works either on the leisure battery as you are travelling along, or on mains electricity if you are plugged in, or on gas if you are not plugged in. Switching from one form of power to the other is challenging, and involves making sure that a whole series of switches are in the right position. To check that the gas is working in the fridge, you have to lie down on the floor and get a severely cricked neck checking for the pilot light, which is hidden at the very back of the inside of the fridge. This is another reason that we like to park up, if at all possible, somewhere where there is an electric hook-up, which assures you that the beer will remain cold and the cheese won't go mouldy.

All of the above systems contain myriad things that can break or go wrong. But a possibly more important element to a camper van is that it needs to drive, and it was with a carefree heart that I decided to take Polly out for a little spin, prior to getting her ready for our trip. I turned the ignition key and … silence. Luckily, my handyman friend Gary was nearby and ready to stroke his chin and shake his head, as he pronounced that the battery was so completely buggered that I'd have to go and buy a new one. A visit to Halfords naturally produced the result that the battery I required was the most expensive one on its shelves and I emerged with a very heavy battery but a light wallet. Still, I comforted myself, at least it's a brand new battery and unlikely to need replacing any time soon. The fact that the engine was now able to start allowed me to take a little trip up to the caravan shop and buy two brand new canisters of gas, certainly enough to last the six weeks we planned to be away.

All in all, I was beginning to feel a little smug, as I called the number of a man who offered a service called a "habitation check", which is a general health check up for a camper van, highly recommended before setting off on a long journey. I was slightly taken aback by his quoted price of £175, but there was no point in scrimping, I'd be sure to regret it if I didn't have it done. The gentleman duly arrived and disappeared inside the van while I retreated into the house. A mere 45 minutes later, he knocked on the door and announced that everything was fine. I knew that it wasn't, because the control panel showing water and battery levels had stopped working, and I'd expected that to be the first thing he mentioned.

"Oh, that." He shrugged. "Yeah, it's broken."

"Is there anything that can be done?"

"Dunno. You could try eBay, I guess."

And that was that. As I returned from the post office where I'd had to pick up £175 in cash (he didn't take cheques), he launched, unprovoked, into a long monologue about all his friends who had recently died before adding, almost casually,

"Oh, by the way, you need four new tyres."

"What? But we've hardly done any miles. The tread is almost new."

"Ah, well, that's the problem. Because the van's been sitting here all winter, the rubber has perished."

"Is it dangerous?"

"Well, for a start, it'll fail its MOT. Plus …" in a sepulchral tone, "… you can take the risk, of course, but if you had a blow-out at seventy miles an hour on the motorway, you'd be unlikely to survive."

That was enough for me, but to be safe, I consulted handyman Gary, who, once again, just happened to be painting the neighbour's fence nearby. He was chatting to another friend of practical bent. Both of them immediately commenced chin-stroking, confirmed the perished rubber theory and the MOT failure, and spookily added,

"Of course, if you had a blow-out at seventy miles an hour on the motorway, you'd be unlikely to survive."

On the other hand, both of them assured me that new tyres would be cheap as anything, probably not more than thirty pounds or so each. Gulp … but of course it was a small price to pay for not being hurled across a motorway by a blow-out. So off I set on a tour of local tyre fitting establishments.

Everyone I spoke to recommended a different one, and there seemed to be one on almost every corner, something I hadn't really noticed before. All of them agreed on one thing: Polly Pocket was a van, not a car, and thus needed special tyres costing a minimum of eighty pounds each. The best price I could get was £320, until the final place I tried, where the semi-comatose young receptionist announced that they could get some discounted ones and that they could therefore do the job for £280. It was still a severe financial blow, but that blow-out image was quite haunting.

"Okay, done."

"We'll ring you as soon as they're in stock."

The call came through early the next day.

"Good morning, Mr Gray. We're happy to say that the tyres are in stock. Bring the van in and we'll fit them."

"Great, thanks."

"Oh, er, by the way, we couldn't get the discount ones, so the price will be £320."

"What? I specifically chose your company because you offered me the best price and now you're casually telling me you're going back on your offer."

"Nothing we can do about it."

In uncharacteristically Meldrewish manner, I uttered the pompous words, "In that case, I shall take my custom elsewhere", and slammed down the phone.

It wasn't until I had calmed down a little that I realized I wouldn't get a better deal anywhere else, so might as well try and make the best of it. I rang back and pointed out that they really did owe it to me to be a little flexible, and in the end, we agreed that they'd do it for a compromise figure of £300.

Now things really were looking great on the mechanical front. Brand new tyres, a brand new battery, two brand new gas canisters and even a brand new water filter. Now we really were good to go. Except that, ninety minutes after returning home from the tyre place, I got a call from my building society.

"Have you recently ordered these items online: £120 worth of clothes from Next and £80 worth of cookery items from Habitat?"

"Certainly not. What's going on?"

"Your credit card has been skimmed, sir."

"Shit, what can I do about that?"

"We'll have to issue you with a new one. It will take four working days to get to you."

"But we're about to set off for six weeks in Europe, and we'll be entirely dependent on using my credit card."

"I'm sorry, sir, there's nothing we can do."

Just a minute … it was Monday, so maybe, just maybe, the card would arrive on Friday, the day we were due to set off. But it'd be touch and go.

Have you noticed? Chapter One is already over, and we still haven't left home.

2

BACK PAGES

Now I'm going to attempt to fit a summary of three European trips into one chapter. Trip Number Four was to be The Big One, but leading up to that came three previous forays. The first one started in Ireland on the way to France, which sounds daft because it's completely the wrong direction. But amazingly, there is a ferry from Rosslare to Cherbourg. It takes nineteen hours but it's dead cheap. And there was a little matter of a music festival to attend in Kilkenny.

From the start, it looked as if the whole trip was going to be a disaster, because I fell ill. Out of nowhere, I contracted a virus that had horrible symptoms that those of a queasy disposition might like to skip. It consisted of uncontrollable coughing fits combined with gallons of phlegm. And worse, the coughing fits led to frequent vomiting. It started in Wales, where the friend we visited witnessed me having to move bedrooms because I was making the bed shake so much. Her recently deceased husband had been a GP, so she had drawers full of medicines, several of which I took with me when we left the next morning, but none of them helped. I was cringing with embarrassment on several occasions at gigs in Kilkenny as I failed to make it through the crowds to the toilet and would end up throwing up on the floor. Pitying looks showed that people merely thought I was an abject drunk. If only. It was the only time I've ever been in Ireland and not been able to drink any Guinness.

It got worse when we arrived in France to spend the night with some old friends. They had prepared an elaborate dinner, which consisted of langoustines (yum) and under-cooked duck (yuck). I had to rush out mid-meal and puke it all up in their flower bed. I don't think they noticed at the time but the evidence the next day must have been incontrovertible.

There was nothing for it but to visit a doctor. In the quaint little village surgery, the GP looked up my symptoms on his iPhone (I could have done that myself but somehow it had more authority when he did it, and anyway, he only charged me twenty euros). He prescribed me two different treatments: a week's course of steroids (Christ, I'm not doing the Tour De France, I thought) and then, to be moved on to if the steroids didn't work, two five-day courses of antibiotics. The steroids duly failed to work and it took both courses of antibiotics to finally clear it up, by which time we were three weeks into the journey and I'd lost over a stone. Did it spoil things? Not at all. Birgit has good quality earplugs and the places we visited were so nice that it didn't really matter that I was feeling shit.

After Ireland, we went through France, Italy, Austria, Luxembourg, Germany and Belgium. But it was Italy that stole our hearts, despite some dodgy campsite experiences. One near Genoa was sandwiched between a railway line and a motorway, while the beach it advertised was a few jagged black rocks. In general, the descriptions seldom matched the reality. The site in Riccione, for example, described itself as "quiet and with direct access to the beach". That actually meant that the beach was attained only by crossing a very busy and noisy highway. But it didn't matter much, because the beach was being dug up by JCBs anyway.

One site was particularly sweet, a small petting farm near the Amalfi Coast. Rather than try to do battle with the brutal traffic that characterises this otherwise idyllic area, we opted for a small farm inland and commuted to the coast by very cheap but massively unpunctual buses. This didn't spoil the fun of eating the home-grown food, drinking the home-made limoncello and petting the kittens and puppies.

One site stood out above all the rest. We arrived at San Felice Circeo in May 12, our 35th wedding anniversary, only to find (for the only time on the trip) that the chosen site was in fact closed. Worrying that we'd spend the fateful evening wild camping beside a highway somewhere, we mooched along the seafront for a bit and spotted a handwritten sign indicating a campsite. This turned out to be an entirely independent operation, run by the charming Raphaelo, who had twelve goats and forty-seven cats among the many other creatures on his small field. He plied us with home-made jam and gave Birgit an anniversary rose, before directing us to the only open local restaurant. It wasn't quite the gourmet experience I'd had in mind, but it did the job.

On we travelled, including a day out on the island of Capri. Here we experienced a familiar tourist phenomenon: The port and main streets were rammed with visitors, but as we walked down the lane to the Blue Grotto, it thinned out until there was almost no one around. The grotto was an amazing experience, although perhaps less so for claustrophobia sufferers, as you have to bend double even to get into it, in the little wooden rowing boats that transport you.

Another day was spent in rain-sodden Naples. Far from experiencing the famed "edgy" atmosphere, we were forced to spend the day sheltering in the Archaeological Museum. This was actually great, because it contained numerous artefacts from Pompeii, where we were positioned on an extraordinary campsite just outside its gates. We'd been recommended two special restaurants where we could have experienced authentic Neapolitan pizza – but both were closed.

On the way home, we spent several days with Antonio Gramentieri, a well-known Italian musician, who has his home and studio in beautiful Modigliana. The surrounding countryside is dedicated to the cultivation of ... guess what, kiwi fruit. By no means indigenous to Northern Italy, this is an EU initiative that has brought great prosperity to the area. Nearby is Faenza, where we once again sheltered from the rain in a museum, this time the incredible Ceramics Museum, which has impressive works by the likes of Pablo Picasso.

Returning up through France was bitter-sweet, as it was during the aftermath of the Charlie-Hebdo killings in Paris. Also, the Brexit referendum was due soon after we got home. Stopping at a military graveyard in Normandy made me almost sick with grief, as the folly of nationalism was laid bare for all to see - or, as it turned out, apparently not. Little did we think that, before long, Birgit would, after forty years in England, have to apply for "permission to remain", and that we would have to obtain (and pay for) international driving permits in order to be allowed to continue our adventures.

In Year Two, we set off a couple of days later than intended because my eldest sister, Faith, died and her funeral was held after we had planned to leave. The funeral was in Gloucestershire, so we camped on a site in a sweet village called Duntisbourne Abbotts. In the evening, we went into Cirencester and had dinner with my nephew Richard, his wife Veronika and their daughter Klara, over from Zürich for the funeral. The funeral took place the next morning near Gloucester. It was a beautiful day and the ceremony and lunch afterwards presented a good opportunity for a family gathering to remember her. It wasn't a fearfully sad occasion, because Faith had been ill with dementia for many years, so in a way it was a blessing for her, but of course it was a rather sombre start to the trip.

We hit the road and Birgit had to drive for nearly six hours to a very hard-to-find campsite on the edge of Dover. Their showers weren't working but it didn't matter, as we had a crack-of-dawn ferry to catch. As our schedule was running late, we took the decision to just drive as far as possible before Birgit got too tired. The day went incredibly well. The intention had been to spend two nights en route for the Mosel but we made it in just one day, pulling into the pretty riverside village of Pommern, where the pre-season campsite was almost deserted. We were spending the money we'd saved up from air BnB guests and were able to have loads of meals out because the other expenses were so low. We walked into the village and were happy to find just one restaurant open. Called Onkel Otto, it served blissful Spargel (fresh white asparagus).

The person we visited in Frankfurt was Elke, an old classmate of Birgit's. As a result of a rather complicated marriage break-up, she now lives in a palatial flat in the heart of Frankfurt, where we were able to park the van and take the lift up to the second-floor apartment. Elke was on sparkling form and lots of reminiscing and laughing went on. The next morning was spent in the nearby *Palmengarten*, before Birgit and I set out on a walking tour of central Frankfurt. We then took the S-Bahn to visit my very old friend Jochen Schmidt (I first met him in 1968). He and his partner Vicky took us to a Greek restaurant owned by a friend of theirs and it naturally turned into an evening of massive hilarity and much alcohol.

The following day was important, as it was our 36th wedding anniversary. As a teenager, I'd visited Rothenburg ob der Tauber and I'd always promised to take Birgit there one day. This was the opportunity. It's hard to describe the beauty of this incredible place, its unspoilt alleys like something straight out of a Grimm's fairy tale. What's more, I had found out that the best hotel in town had been owned by the parents of my Berlin rock critic friend H-P Daniels. It was clear we'd have to stay there, and so it transpired – in a turreted attic room in the annexe over the road, which felt like a private house.

A gorgeous day was in store. We wandered round the idyllic wooden-roofed city walls and stopped for beer in a *Strandkorb* in a beautiful, secluded *Biergarten* before searching for a restaurant out of the many on offer. Clearly, it had to be the perfect one for such an occasion, and so it turned out, as we found a cosy, very authentic *Gasthof*, complete with busty waitresses in Dirndls. Afterwards, we had a schnapps in the bar of the Hotel Eisenhut, where we drank a toast to H-P Daniels beneath a portrait of his grandfather in the very room where H-P had been christened. It had been a wonderful day, made better by that feeling of comfort I always get in Germany, where life seems so orderly and timeless.

In the morning, after a browse through Käthe Wohlfahrt's Christmas shop, we returned to the Romantic Road. It's not meant to be romantic in the lovey-dovey sense (although it does feel like it) but rather in the atmospheric sense of romantic literature and Gothic architecture. The road meanders delightfully through the undulating landscape and picture-perfect villages, all still equipped with a bakery, an ice cream parlour and at least one bank. The brown tourist route signs can be slightly confusing because they point both north and south but don't say which is which. More than once, we found ourselves exiting a village the way we had entered it just minutes before.

Next up was Dinkelsbühl, a gorgeously unspoilt jumble of medieval half-timbered buildings that we explored in a covered horse and carriage, to avoid the rain. An even more delightful surprise was Nördlingen, whose town walls are as intact as those of Rothenburg. You can get a unique panoramic view of them and miles of surrounding countryside from the dizzy heights of the church, which has its own cat that guards the tower. It's breathtaking in more ways than one.

Augsburg is the biggest city on the southern end of the Romantic Road. It's the birthplace of Bertolt Brecht, and we spent an hour the next morning in the small but gripping museum that charts his intriguing life story. Nearby is the *Fuggerei*, the oldest social housing complex in the world. Created by the philanthropist Jakob Fugger, it is still dedicated to the welfare of the poor in the area. In this spirit, we sneaked in without paying.

The next day we found, rising up from a field shortly before Füßen, the World Heritage site of the Wieskirche. It's an extraordinarily ornate Catholic church dating from 1740, covered with colourful frescoes and gold decorations. The crowning glories we discovered at the end of the Romantic Road were the twin castles of Hohenschwangau and Neuschwanstein, the latter being the gigantic and hugely impressive brainchild of "Mad" King Ludwig II of Bavaria, and the model for Disney's cartoon castles. You can observe this unique and almost unbelievable building from a slightly rickety bridge that is not advised for vertigo sufferers but is definitely worth the risk. After checking out a rainy and largely deserted Oberammergau, we spent the night in Lechbruck am See in a raging storm that threatened to blow the van over.

A spectacular drive over the Gerls-Pass took us the poshest campsite ever, in a place called Bruch. The toilet block (complete with heating and piped music) was like a Las Vegas hotel, and it also boasted a spectacular mini-golf course. Bruch is at the bottom of the *Großglockner*, a thrilling mountain pass that exists pretty much just as a tourist attraction. Certainly nobody uses it as a road to get from A to B (as there is a 35 euro toll fee). Motorcyclists love it and there are little museums to stop at en route to the gigantic glacier. It was a day of brilliant sunshine and, at the top, we had a delicious *Leberknödelsuppe* in the panoramic restaurant.

Now we were well on the way to Lake Bled, accessed by yet another mountain pass, this time the Wurzenpass into Slovenia. At Lake Bled, we were booked into a 5 star (but still cheap) campsite by the lake. Gorgeous sunshine ruled as we did all the tourist stuff (rowing to the island, hiking to the castle, eating the local cream cake). It was a surreal time because we had internet on the campsite and were rapidly realizing that Theresa May was royally cocking up her election campaign. It felt strange but exciting to be so far from the action, yet getting a sense of something amazing going on at home.

One day, we caught a local bus to the nearby Lake Blini, where we took the precipitous cable car to the Vogel mountain. You are deposited near the top and can hike on up towards the summit, which we did, accompanied by a herd of extremely friendly (not to say randy and ravenous) goats. I adore random train trips and the next day, we walked up to the station and took the decrepit, slow but very cheap train to Ljubljana, where we explored the city and took the funicular up to the castle.

Then came a day of three thirds. A walk along the craggy Vintgar gorge was followed by the hairiest mountain pass adventure yet, along the so-called Russian Road. This pass was vertiginous, narrow and largely cobbled and potholed, with forty-nine hairpin bends on each side, but with unbelievable views and unhindered by traffic, as no one else was mad enough to attempt it. We then ended up driving endlessly through very drab northern Italian industrial areas, before eventually finding a campsite by a beautiful lake, which had the advantage of the cheapest restaurant in existence - the glorious pizzas cost four euros each and half a litre of Prosecco was two euros. We were, however, bitten to death by mosquitoes, and thus spent the next day attending to bites and blisters.

As we left the campsite the next morning, we were offered some Prosecco by the owner, who explained that we were on the edge of the Prosecco region, which we hadn't realised. Sure enough, within minutes, we found ourselves driving through lovely countryside along the *Strada del Prosecco*. Determined to find some more to buy, we entered a village and spotted a shop called *Emporio Superiore*. At first it seemed we'd be disappointed, because it hadn't yet opened and was still in the process of being decorated. But the young proprietor, Jean-Michel, welcomed us in and treated us to a tasting and a talk about the different types of Prosecco. We left with a box of Prosecco bottles and the feeling of having made a friend for life.

The drive to Verona was long and dull, but we were rewarded by a beautiful little camp site overlooking the city, filled with aromatic flowers. We wandered down the steep steps into the centre, taking in Juliet's house (and balcony) and a posh aperitif. The next day was spent as full-on tourists, viewing the cathedral, the tower, the art museum, the castle, the bridge and the river, and taking in an over-priced meal and a Pink Floyd tribute band in the amphitheatre that the campsite overlooked.

We'd reached the stage of long drives now, with a ferry deadline to hit, so it was another full-on driving day, enlivened by nearly running out of diesel near Lake Como, having a picnic on the shore and ending up at yet another beautiful lake, Lake Piano, where a super-cool young Swiss guy said little Polly Pocket was the best camper van he'd ever seen. I was bursting with pride.

The next stop was Switzerland, entailing a very long mountain motorway drive from Lugano. We were rewarded by a warm welcome in Zürich from Richard and Veronika, who had read on Facebook about the blisters I had incurred on our various hikes, and had bought me some very soothing and effective remedies.

The next day, we faced another long drive, this time all the way to Haspelschied in Alsace, through endless vineyards in baking heat, ending up at the home of Dominique, a teacher of English who we had first met in 1983. In the morning, we walked to the local lake for baguette and croissants, before the Sat Nav inadvertently led us through deep woods on tiny lanes to yet another slightly shabby and almost deserted lakeside campsite, conveniently situated next to one of my favourite things, a run-down and desolate fun park called "Elfiland".

For Year Three, we decided to head for Northern Spain, for no better reason than that a friend had recommended it. We bought a book detailing back road routes, which made for a really authentic experience.

The ferry from Portsmouth brought us to Santander, from where it was a short drive to Altamira, for the extraordinary prehistoric cave paintings, then an amazing town called Comillas, where there are numerous examples of Antoni Gaudí's architecture. His *El Capricho* is an incredible villa that was built by him between 1883 and 1885 as the summer residence for a wealthy patron, Máximo Díaz de Quijano. It features extraordinarily ornate multicoloured glazed ceramic tile work and stained glass. We had had no idea that Gaudí had produced any work outside Catalonia, so the whole thing was a total surprise. Oddly, Gaudí, who was only 31, never visited his creation and didn't even meet the person who commissioned it. Even more sadly, Máximo never got to enjoy his home, as he died before its completion.

A gateway by the town's main car park is a witty Gaudí creation that has three entrances, one for pedestrians, one for animals and one for birds to fly though. An evening meal on the campsite revealed that you could have a three-course feast, including half a litre of wine, for eleven euros, something we proceeded to do on virtually every evening of the trip.

Continuing through Cantabria on the way to a campsite at Foz, we visited the *Playa de las Catedrales* and the next day drove along the coast, seeing beautiful villages and, rather confusingly, two different places called Ortigueira. We got revenge for the tattered state of the campsite by conning them into thinking we'd only stayed one night rather than two.

Following suggestions in the guidebook, we travelled through a succession of lovely but completely deserted villages, many of which had numerous abandoned buildings. We ended up, for the only time in the entire three years, on an *Aire*, which was a municipal campsite with minimal facilities. It seemed fine, until the issue of where to go to the loo cropped up. There was nowhere.

The Picos mountains were spectacularly attractive, easily on a par with the Alps, and we visited deserted mountain villages, continually crossing the *Camino de Santiago*, until reaching the campsite at the coastal town of Ribadessella, which had the unexpected luxury of an indoor heated pool. The Picos offered mountain passes, winding roads, snow, rocky gorges, valleys, tunnels, blue sky and sunshine. We almost decided to stay in a hotel in one of the many idyllic villages which only had one road in and out, but in the end drove to Potes, a gorgeous tourist town near to the Santo Toribio monastery and the very steep and high cable car up to Fuente Dé. I thoughtlessly ascended wearing shorts and a T-shirt and couldn't understand why the other passengers were wrapped up in ski gear, until we reached the summit and found there was a foot of snow. Shiver! In the evening, there was some kind of festival going on in Potes, which featured a spectacular light show on the central tower and an opera performed, mid-air, on bikes. Fireworks were exploding all around as we walked back to the campsite.

More adventures followed the next day, in the form of a visit to a tiny mountain village, famous for its unique cheese. Of course, we bought some very smelly samples from a farm, but never actually got around to eating any of them, as they really were just too smelly. On my insistence, we ascended the extraordinarily expensive EU-funded funicular, which was the only way to get to Bulnes, the most remote village in the Picos.

Now it was time for some City activity. A waterlogged campsite outside Bilbao was at least near a bus route into the centre, and we had a cultural day out in the Guggenheim art museum. The next day took us to an obscurely-situated site just outside San Sebastián, where the proprietor offered the service of driving campers into the city in a minibus. That allowed us to indulge in some sensational *Pintxos* and a few beers.

The next day, a nice hike in the National Park relieved the tedium of some horrible lorry-dominated roads on the way to Pamplona, which disappointingly featured no running bulls but plenty of references to Ernest Hemingway. The skies above the gorge at Foz de Lumbia were filled with vultures, and soon we were heading through the snowy Pyrenees, eventually arriving at Lourdes, frankly one of the most bizarre places I have ever encountered. Of course, we had to visit St Bernadette's grotto and try the Holy Water, while observing the bedraggled pilgrims, some of them lying on hospital trolleys, hoping to be cured while being assailed by a violent hailstorm. "They'll catch their death of cold," I thought, irreverently. One surprising feature of the pilgrimage site was that it had the filthiest, most evil toilets either of us had ever experienced anywhere in the world.

We were headed for the French coast, but nothing could have prepared us for the gigantic sand dunes at Pila, which surely ought to be one of the Wonders Of The World. We nearly killed ourselves climbing the precipitous walls of sand, to be rewarded by close-up encounters with the daredevil paragliders. The tourist town of Arcachon was just nearby, so we indulged in an overpriced meal and caught a ferry over to Cap Ferret for a little mini-train ride.

Neither of us had ever been to Bordeaux, and we didn't have much in the way of expectations, thinking that it would probably be a bit like Portsmouth, but we found a campsite nearby and managed to create a sensational home-made dinner of prawns and asparagus. In the morning, a local bus took us into the city, providing much entertainment in the form of a very demonstrative, angry, gesticulating (but rather sexy) female driver. Bordeaux was delightful, not in the least like Portsmouth.

Then it was on to the Dordogne, staying outside the charming town of Sarlat, where I took an *ascenseur panoramique* to the top of the church tower. In Martel, the "town of the seven towers", we found a rustic vintage steam train, but when we got back to Sarlat, we found that someone had nicked our pitch, despite the fact that we had left a chair and table firmly on it, in order to deter interlopers.

On the way to visit friends near Limoges, we had the joyful experience of stumbling across a completely unexpected gem, in the form of the Château de Pompadour, which turned out to be the National Stud. Here, we watched a very informative video about artificial insemination. The gallons of sperm produced by the stallions are quite impressive.

With our friends Tim and Sally, we were able to celebrate our 37th wedding anniversary in one of my favourite restaurants in the world, the *Cheval Blanc* in Bellac, where the proprietor is so spectacularly aloof and condescending that you either love him or hate him. Personally, I love him.

All in all, after three years and many, many miles, we felt we were experienced and well-enough prepared to undertake a bigger trip. How wrong could we have been?

---(3)---

THE BIG ONE

Now it was time for The Big One, to Sicily and back, and all points in between.

As it was going to be impossible to have the traditional wedding anniversary meal on the actual anniversary (which would be spent on a campsite near Lewes), we decided to postpone it until reaching France. For now, the itinerary decreed that we would head towards Newhaven, in order to take the crossing to Dieppe. The reasoning behind choosing that route dated back to the days when Brexit was set to take place on March 31st, and we reasoned that a quieter port than Dover was less likely to have descended into chaos. It would also take us more in the direction we wanted to go, namely the Champagne region of France.

Lewes … it's one of those classic English town names that you're never sure how to pronounce, like Totnes. Maybe it's Lewze? But no, it's okay, it's pronounced quite sensibly, like Kevin Whateley's Oxford detective. As it lay exactly between Newhaven and the chosen campsite, it was an ideal place to head to for the afternoon tea which was to temporarily replace anniversary celebrations.

Some things I knew about Lewes were that it is quaint, has a castle and a terrifying firework obsession. It has also become home to many young creative people who can no longer afford to live in London. One example of this kind of culture is a unique little record store in the centre of town, which was our initial target as we entered East Sussex. We stopped off at Union Records for a chat with the proprietor and to pick his brains on the subject of nice tea shops in Lewes. Extraordinarily, he seemed to have little knowledge on such a vital matter, so we headed for the pretty High Street, where we found a plethora of tea establishments and were able to conduct an initial anniversary celebration by galumphing egg and cress doorstep sandwiches and toasted tea cakes.

It was only twenty minutes or so to the campsite that we had booked in advance. It wasn't an ACSI campsite, because there are hardly any of them in the UK. Instead, we had discovered that the only way to get camping discount is to join something called the Camping and Caravanning Club. This also turned out to be a disappointment, because most campsites under that banner are relatively primitive affairs on small farms. Unfortunately, rather like with the National Trust and English Heritage, it turns out that there are two major UK camping organisations. The other one is called the Caravan and Motorhome Club. Inevitably, any nice sites that we find online turn out to belong to that one. If you aren't a member, the prices are so high as to be unfeasible. You might as well park outside the Travelodge and sleep there.

The site we eventually identified was completely independent and didn't seem to belong to any of those chains. When I rang up to reserve a place, I was rather surprised to hear a thick Glaswegian accent on the other end of the phone, but it was an extremely friendly voice that welcomed me to book for the allotted night. A pleasant drive through the East Sussex countryside took us to the site, where the gentleman I had spoken to was waiting to greet us.

When I meet people I immediately like, I tend to ask what their names are, which is what I did on this occasion.

"Greem."

"Sorry?"

"Greem."

"Oh Graham! Hi Graham, is there anywhere nearby where we could have a quiet drink? It's our wedding anniversary."

"Aye, there's the Beestra."

"Pardon?"

"The Beestra."

"Ah, the Bistro!"

No wonder I hadn't got that one. The thought of a bijou bistro here in the wilds of the Sussex countryside was so unlikely that I assumed I must have mis-heard. Anyway, even if there was a bistro, surely, with our luck, it would be bound to be closed.

It was very much pre-season and the campsite was sparsely populated. Graham invited us to park anywhere we wanted, so we drove into the middle of a large field and plugged in to the nearest electricity post.

Then came the setting-up ritual that has to be undertaken on arrival each day. First you have to wind down the legs at the back of the van that contribute to it being level and stable. This entails lying on your back with a large spanner-like device, an activity that is relatively straightforward as long as the ground isn't muddy, in which case you have to spread out a plastic sheet (and then subsequently clean it, yuck). Next, you open the little cupboard and switch on the gas supply. Finally, inside the van, you throw a few switches in order to turn on the hot water boiler.

In view of all the preparations we'd done, I was relatively confident that things ought to be in working order, so it was a surprise and a major shock when water immediately began pouring out of Polly's bottom. In a panic, and acting totally illogically, I assumed that the tap at the bottom of the water tank must have been switched on and rushed to turn it off. This was a terrible move because, within seconds, I found myself standing holding the tap, which had become detached from the outlet pipe. Looking at it in horror and despair, it was clear that the connection had rusted away.

All I could think of doing was returning to Graham in the camp reception to ask if he knew anyone nearby who could carry out a repair. Unsurprisingly, as it was way past shop closing time, he was unable to help and assured me that there was no one suitable anyway. I briefly wondered about casting around in the morning but then remembered that the ferry was due to leave at 8 a.m.

The problem was quite a severe one, because you can do very little in a camper van without a supply of water, yet the only way to retain any water in the tank is to have a closed tap attached to it. The tank was of course now empty. I had no idea whether or not Graham was of a practical bent, but, being in such a pickle, I plucked up courage to ask if he could come and have a look at it. Together, we trudged across the field, where Graham did quite a lot of tut-tutting before announcing - oh joy - that he thought he had the solution.

As we returned to the reception, Graham explained that there had been a recent change of ownership of the campsite. Normally there would be a fully equipped workshop on site, but the previous owners had taken everything away with them. Nonetheless, he was going to take a look in the workshop to see if he could find anything that might help.

What happened next may sound like something I have invented, but I promise it is true in every respect. We entered the workshop, which was lined with empty shelves, yet in the middle of one of them there was a single item: a small plastic tap.

"That'll do," said Graham, and gave it to me.

"That's fantastic, but what am I supposed to do with it?"

"Undo the jubilee clip, attach the tap and do the jubilee clip up again." (I won't attempt the Scottish phonetics.)

It sounded so simple that I jogged back to the van with a spring in my step. My extremely limited tool kit did indeed contain a screwdriver, but not the Phillips screwdriver that was required to tackle the jubilee clip. After another visit to Graham, I returned with the correct screwdriver and attempted to unscrew the completely rusted-up offending item. There was of course no way in a million years that it was going to come undone and certainly no way in another million years then it would ever be in a fit condition to do up again.

Back I went to Graham, increasingly fearing that he would be getting fed up with me and leave us to our fate, but so indefatigability cheerful was he, that he accompanied me back to the van in order to have a go himself. When it was apparent that not even he could achieve the impossible, he invited me to drive Polly over to the workshop. This, of course, entailed switching off the gas, winding up the legs and unplugging the electricity, but there wasn't really any alternative.

At the workshop, Graham changed into some overalls, laid out sheets on the floor and disappeared under Polly's skirts armed with some kind of angle grinder, with which he proceeded to attack the offending pipe. All we could see was his legs and a display of sparks worthy of an Einstürzende Neubauten concert. It took about half an hour, but eventually the brand new tap had been attached with a brand new jubilee clip and Graham emerged triumphant, holding up his hands and refusing to accept any kind of payment.

"But surely you'll let us give you a bottle of wine at least?"

"Aim teetle."

"Pardon?"

"Aim teetle."

"Oh, you're teetotal?"

All I could do was re-emphasise my abject state of gratefulness and assure him that his site would be receiving the world's greatest ever Trip Advisor review.

To add to the joy, we then ambled up the road and were amazed to find that there was indeed a delightful bistro, overlooking a small fishing lake. They were no longer serving food, but at least we were able to toast the anniversary with lager as the sun dipped below the trees and the ducks quacked around us. It was time to reflect, not for the last time, that for every piece of bad luck, there is normally a piece of good and behind that, there will normally be a good, kind, honourable person.

Newhaven turned out to be a fine choice of embarkation point. The approaches to most channel ports are along dismal roads through bleak industrial areas, whereas the road to Newhaven is along bucolic country lanes and the pier is next to a traditional port and beach. The check-in was swift, friendly and almost entirely lacking in security.

The crossing was just as you'd expect out of season. Fellow passengers consisted of a few lorry drivers, a coachload of pensioners and a couple of cyclists. Birgit gets seasick, so our ferry routine is an odd one. No remedy has worked, except for one that a friend recommended to her, consisting of fixing her eyes on the horizon for the entire journey. This entails us immediately rushing to the front of the ship in order to bag a forward-facing window seat, followed by me reading the paper and doing crosswords, while Birgit stares straight ahead. This must look odd, because we do in fact converse but don't look at each other while doing so.

On arrival in Dieppe, the route snaked up a grassy hill and straight onto a country road that was the start of our drive to Soissons, where the first night was to be spent. Soissons ... ah, what a beautiful-sounding French word, it rolls off the tongue like a hissing serpent. I felt blissfully happy, as I always do when leaving the UK for practically anywhere else, but especially France. We'd told our Sat Nav to "avoid motorways", so the route was the traditional one of deserted villages and tree-lined avenues, with the occasional lake or château in the distance. Of traffic there was little sign.

The campsite was bathed in sunshine as we arrived. We were greeted with great warmth by owners Gérard and Sylvie, who explained that they were doing their pre-season preparations and that we could park up anywhere we wanted, as - get this - they only had one other guest. As I looked around, that wasn't strictly true. All campsites everywhere seem to have one or two permanent residents, people who never leave. The tell-tale sign is the odd tumbledown, algae-covered caravan in amongst all the pristine ones. Back on Graham's site there'd been one of those. Graham had cheerfully explained that it was an old man who'd turned up one day years before and never left. When he ran out of money, they just let him stay on regardless, as part of the furniture, because they felt sorry for him. There were a couple of these on the Soissons site.

Gérard reacted with alacrity to my need to speak as much French as possible, and we had a long and lively conversation as he continued his work on preparing the swimming pool. He had to clean everything, paint it twice, fill it, empty it, treat it with chemicals, fill it again, empty it again, then monitor it for a week before he could open it to the public.

Gérard and Sylvie had recently bought the site, having quit their jobs working for the Carrefour supermarket chain. They claimed that this new lifestyle was much less stressful, but it looked tough. There was a hell of a lot to do before the season started in a few weeks. Gérard gave me his bike and invited me to ride around the site. It was huge, with rows of slightly shabby chalets, a playground and a large lake bursting with enormous carp. We ordered our croissants for the morning, cooked some pasta (it was well before restaurant opening season) and settled down in Polly to watch a DVD.

The technique we use for watching DVDs is to position ourselves on our beds and plonk a cushion between us. The tiny DVD player sits on top of the cushion until one of us presses play. The volume is extremely low, so you have to listen very carefully and concentrate. The box set that we had chosen was a collection of early stories about Inspector Montalbano. This burly but rather enigmatic police inspector lives and operates in a fictitious Sicilian port called Vigàta. Each episode is a couple of hours long and features a bunch of eccentric colleagues and Salvo Montalbano's pneumatic girlfriend Livia in some rather entertaining sex scenes. Crimes are committed in various parts of Sicily and Salvo invariably solves them in the last ten minutes. We thought it would be instructive to swot up on Sicily by watching as many episodes as we could before we got there, and indeed we did exactly that every evening along the route to the island.

Our sleeping arrangement in the van, in case you are interested, is separate beds. There is a practical reason for this. We both need to get up in the night for loo visits, especially if beers have been consumed. If I had to clamber over my wife in order to access the Elsan, it would surely wake her up, and then she would take hours to get back to sleep. As it is, we both sleep like logs on the very narrow banquettes and don't interfere with each other's movements.

Every French campsite has the facility to order croissants and baguettes and at nine a.m., as agreed, Sylvie was knocking on the door with the *délices*. The hit of your first proper French croissant for a year (croissants from anywhere else don't count) is like shooting up when your dealer hasn't delivered for days (at least, I assume that's what it's like). Sure, after a couple more days you'll already be getting fed up (pardon the pun) with them, but for the time being, smeared with the home-made raspberry jam we'd brought with us, they felt like the greatest self-indulgence imaginable. Which indeed they are. *"Pur beurre"*, they are labelled, and pure butter they are, veritable cholesterol bombs that French people somehow manage to consume every day, along with cakes, bread, sauces and wine, and still not put on any weight.

The baguette we ordered each morning played a different role. Every day before setting off, Birgit would create a picnic for us to have for lunch in some convenient lay-by. She would very neatly cut a baguette in two and in one half she would create a meaty sandwich for herself and in the other half a cheesy sandwich for me. Baguettes in France are blissful things but they do have certain characteristics that you have to bear in mind. Firstly, you have to eat them within a few hours of purchase before they go rock hard. Secondly, the type of baguette can vary from region to region. The traditional golden coloured baguette which you can find in most *boulangeries* has a flaky crust and is deliciously crunchy, but its darker-hued and currently fashionable cousin (anything that calls itself *artisanal*) can be brutally hard and sometimes ends in a point that would make it usable as a dagger to attack someone with. The other thing to remember is that, if you're not used to eating several slices of baguette a day, they can cause havoc with your digestive system in the form of (sorry to use the word) constipation.

I need to explain the relevance of the baguette issue. Clearly, the best way to eat a baguette is to sink your teeth into it and rip it apart before masticating it and swallowing it. I, however, was faced with a dental issue which made baguettes highly dangerous items. Three weeks before departure, I was sitting in the kitchen eating an entirely innocuous plate of spaghetti Bolognese, when I realised that my front tooth had fallen out. Well, it wasn't an actual tooth, it was a crown that had been in there for years. A glance in the mirror revealed that I had been transformed into the Jon Pertwee version of Worzel Gummidge, with a Calcutta-like black hole where my glistening front gnasher should have been. Yes, I am indeed extremely vain, but anybody seeing me smile in those circumstances would certainly have fainted in terror.

Luckily, I have a delightful dentist, who glued it back in place with temporary cement and made an appointment for two days before we set off on our trip, to replace the temporary tooth with a proper crown. On the morning of the appointment, I got a call from the surgery:

"Some of our equipment has broken down and we're having to cancel all appointments."

"But we're just about to leave on holiday and I will be confronted with baguettes every day."

"I'm afraid you'll have to stay clear of baguettes, as your temporary tooth is very fragile and could fall out at any moment."

Thus it was that I spent the entire six weeks on the road terrified of finding my tooth embedded in some food item and having to visit a no doubt brutal and very expensive dentist en route. A new baguette tackling technique needed to be invented. Each lunchtime, I would have to use my fingers to break off a small corner of the sandwich, insert it in the side of my mouth and chew it gently and cautiously, without letting it go anywhere near the vulnerable incisor. It meant, in general, much less pleasure from baguette gnawing but also a consequent reduction in constipation.

We set off along a country route that would eventually take us to the mediaeval city of Troyes, which was our target for that day. The Sat Nav gives you the option of choosing to avoid motorways, and, unless you're in a hurry, this is always a good method for finding scenic routes. Another thing you can do, if you have the patience, is look at a map in advance and make a list of the towns you'd like to pass through. Then, as you progress, you can just insert the next town into the machine.

As usual in France, the roads took us through a succession of nondescript but nonetheless delightful villages. The roads tend to go straight through the middle of these settlements, but are very efficiently curbed by suitably vicious traffic calming devices such as sharp chicanes, mountainous sleeping policemen and flashing LED lights showing a smiley face if you are obeying the speed limit and a glum one if you are not. Each village has an impressive white stone *mairie* with crossed *tricolores* over the door, plus normally a huge and ornate church of some kind and several *boulangeries*, some of which are closed down and boarded up. One major change in recent years has been the arrival also of at least one kebab shop in each village. The UK equivalent is the Chinese takeaway that can be found in every small town.

At the edge of each town can be found a *supermarché*, sometimes combined with a petrol station. These can take the form of a *Super U*, an *Intermarché*, a *Carrefour*, an *Auchan* or one of a further selection of chains. On the way to Troyes, we noticed that the plastic lid that covers the electrical hook-up on the side of the van was flapping in the wind, so the local Carrefour came in very useful as we stopped and purchased probably the world's biggest pack of Blu-Tak to stick it back down with. This has the advantage of meaning we will probably never need to buy any more Blu-Tak as long as we live.

I don't know what it is about French supermarkets, but they fill me with a feeling of excitement that I certainly don't get from their UK equivalents. I think it has something to do with the fact that the shelves are filled with different things from what you would expect at home, so pushing the trolley around is actually a voyage of discovery. You'd think the attraction would wear off, but it still gets me every time, to the extent that I will request to stop at a supermarket even if we don't actually need to buy anything.

On the way to Troyes, we stopped for coffee in a town called

Sézanne, which happened to be on our route. Discovering random places with unexpected charms is part of the fun of a camper van holiday, and Sézanne delivered in spades, as we strolled around the restored ramparts and explored the tree-lined avenues. At one stage, we stumbled upon a house where Napoleon had stayed on 9 February, 1814. The display board explained the circumstances: The French campaign of 1814 had been Napoleon's last great military achievement. Although the campaign ended with an Allied victory and Napoleon's abdication, he had managed to inflict a series of defeats on the Allied armies invading France. Napoleon arrived at Sézanne with his Imperial Guard after a difficult march along mud-covered roads. Farmers used teams of horses to help pull the cannons through the mire and they moved on from Sézanne after just one night. But it was certainly worth a plaque.

And then it was on to Troyes. Troyes is a city that I would like to tell you more about.

---
(4)

UN, DEUX, TROYES

In 1985, I was teaching languages in Winchester and becoming more and more painfully aware that my French, which I was then required to teach to GCSE level, was becoming distinctly rusty. I therefore applied to go on a teacher exchange. This resulted in me pitching up with Birgit and the two year-old Annabel in the previously completely unknown (to us) city of Troyes, the capital of France's Champagne region. The only reason we ended up in Troyes was that my French opposite number, a teacher who wanted to spend some time in the UK, lived there.

The school was the *Collège Beurnonville*, which, to my horror, looked like a dismal prison, a huge stone edifice in the middle of the city, with tiny windows and an asphalted playground that looked like an exercise yard. The looks belied the truth, however, and I spent a glorious four months having the experience of a lifetime teaching charming and enthusiastic children and being treated like royalty by pupils, colleagues and parents alike.

Mention the city of Troyes to an English person and you'll probably get the response, "I've heard of it but I've never been there." This is because it is efficiently bypassed by the A5 *autoroute*, meaning that anyone travelling South from the channel ports would have seen Troyes on signposts lots of times, but probably won't have stopped off for a visit.

To clear up the first question everyone asks, the pronunciation is as in *un, deux, **Trois*** and not as in Helen of... . As it's the capital of the Champagne region, copious amounts of the sparkling nectar are drunk here, even though the bottling plants and cellars are mainly in nearby Reims. It's a wonderful place to wander around and, because it's not nearly such a tourist magnet as it ought to be, it's pleasantly quiet. Fairytale half-timbered buildings, impeccably restored, cluster round the market place and down the numerous narrow alleyways, the best known of which is the *Ruelle des Chats*, or Cat Alley. The city centre is enclosed within a network of roads which, on a map, exactly resembles a champagne bottle cork and is known as the

Bouchon de Champagne. Here you can stroll from restaurant to bar unhindered by traffic.

Just outside the centre lies the Catholic cathedral, which dates from the twelfth century and contains some of the most stunning stained-glass windows to be found anywhere in France. Just behind the cathedral is the museum of modern art, with a collection of top quality abstract works. The River Seine flows right through the city, and there are also unusual shopping opportunities. The area's main industry is clothing manufacture, so on every corner there are shops selling "seconds", and also a large number of full-scale outlets offering designer clothing at bargain prices. Some of the labels manufactured in the area are *Le Coq Sportif* for sports gear and *Le Petit Bâteau* for children's clothes. Just nearby is the *Forêt d'Orient*, a forested area, rich in wildlife, where we would spend every Sunday picnicking on an artificial beach beside the large lake.

All around the local hills you can find small Champagne vineyards, where you can taste the goods and buy them straight from the source. One of my pupils back then was a young lad called Alex Lassaigne who, despite not being very good at English, took a liking to me and invited us out to meet his parents in the local hilltop village of Montgueux, where they owned a quite prestigious vineyard. We were given a guided tour and presented with several boxes of their Champagne. They also introduced us to the restaurant in the village, where we subsequently dined several times, receiving impeccable service and a very small bill.

If you've ever wondered why Champagne is so expensive, learning about its creation goes a long way towards explaining it. It starts out as normal white table wine. You fill a one-litre bottle with 26 grams of sugar and three percent of starter culture and seal it with the familiar wire top. The bottles are then kept horizontally for six months at exactly 13.3 degrees celsius. After six months, the bottles are given a good shake and are again kept for ageing, at the same temperature, for between six months and four years, depending on what quality you wish to create. After ageing, some precipitate (i.e. gunge) has settled and now needs removing. This is done in a novel way, because you need to get rid of it without losing any CO_2. The bottles are cooled at 4 degrees for one to two weeks, and then you slowly invert them so that the gunge sinks down to the neck. The bottlenecks are then inserted into a chiller at minus fifteen degrees. Now the precipitate is formed into a block of ice. The cork is removed just for an instant and the pressure of the gas blasts out the ice block. The cork is quickly replaced and the champagne is ready for sale.

Despite the care put into its production, everybody in Troyes seemed to drink Champagne as if it was lemonade, and after a few weeks, various parents plucked up courage to invite us round for meals. As our period there drew towards its end, we spent the last two weeks going out for dinner with local families every single evening. While this was incredibly kind, it did present one or two issues. The first one was that they were keen to introduce us to the local culinary delights, one of which was roast duck. I'm not a fan of duck at the best of times, but when you've eaten it every day for a fortnight, it really is a challenge. They thought it was amusing to chop the head off the duck, waving it in the face of the infant Annabel and making quacking noises. They also delighted in inviting us to suck the brains out of the head of the duck, allegedly the most delicious part. It was hard to decline without seeming ungrateful, but decline we did.

None of this seems to have put Annabel off her appetite and to this day, she is an enthusiast for any expensive gourmet meals on offer. Meanwhile, dessert was invariably *tarte aux pommes*, which was delicious but somewhat repetitive. All of it was washed down with lashings of Champagne. It was a complete miracle that I was able to get up in the morning and do any kind of coherent teaching.

So it was with a very intense feeling of nostalgia that we

found ourselves approaching Montgueux, many years after we had last left it. It was impossible to resist the temptation to check out the vineyard and the restaurant, so we ascended the hairpin-bended road and arrived in the middle of the deserted village, where a huge sign and an arrow led us to *Champagne Lassaigne*. We drew into the yard, where a suspicious looking gentleman in overalls approached us. It was clear that they didn't get much passing trade. I explained who I was and that we were on a mission to see what had become of Alex. It turned out that this was his brother Thierry. He explained that father Jacques was no longer alive, that he had taken over the vineyard and that Alex was doing something technological in Paris. So, despite my lack of success in teaching him English, he'd obviously done all right for himself. Thierry, still clearly untrusting of our motives, almost cracked a smile when I asked about the restaurant. Apparently it had closed over twenty years before.

For the next two nights, we were going to be staying with our friend Colette, who had been head of the English department at the *Collège* while I was working there. An utterly delightful person, she had played host to us on numerous occasions back then, when she and her husband were doing up a pretty mediaeval farm building and turning it into a characterful residence for themselves. Not long after the project was completed, the couple split up but, not being able to afford to live apart, simply divided the building into two and lived separate lives in the two halves, continuing to have a perfectly civil relationship.

Colette had lived an interesting life in the interim, working her way up to being a senior teacher trainer in the Champagne region and teaming up with her current partner, who is a very eminent and respected wildlife photographer and artist. Less than a year before we visited, Colette had been struck by a bus in Central Troyes and was lucky to have survived. We parked Polly in the shade of the apple trees in Colette's garden and pretty quickly got stuck into the *apéritifs* which, as always in France, magically appeared on her table.

By way of saying thank you to her, we badly wanted to take her out for a meal, but an extraordinary transformation had taken place in the vicinity of the beautifully named village of Belley, where Colette lives. Back in 1985, it had been a sleepy hamlet outside the city, but in the interim it has been joined to Troyes by a gigantic trading estate, centred round a branch of the E Leclerc hypermarket, which must be the size of Wembley stadium. There's a whole collection of the kind of chain restaurants that you think would never be tolerated in France, but in fact thrive. One of these is the

Belgian mussels chain called *Léon*, which has cleverly taken the fast food concept and applied it to the normally dignified combination of *moules* and *frites*. To my amazement, it was jam-packed with rather deprived-looking families, much like your local McDonald's, but actually was astronomically expensive. This was our first taste of how the shocking pound to euro exchange rate was going to clip our spending wings as we travelled around.

The next day was an unashamed nostalgia trip. We took a bus into and out of town and were able to see at first-hand how easily you could be run over by one, as they were swift, silent and deadly. First, we visited the school, which seemed to have changed not one iota. The children running around in the playground under the watchful eye of the student *pions* (paid supervisors) now looked largely Arabic, whereas before there had been a strong Portuguese contingent. They still seemed extremely well behaved, polite and adult in their behaviour, but I did have to accept that I would no longer have had the energy to keep them alert and occupied for six hour-long lessons a day. We spent an hour or so in the cathedral, having our minds completely blown by the sensationally spectacular stained glass, before spending lunchtime sitting in the dappled sunlight in a cobbled mediaeval street, eating unbelievably delicious *galettes* and sipping locally produced *cidre*. This, at last, was the long-awaited anniversary meal.

In the morning, it was time to move on towards Djion, as the next stage of the long journey to Genoa, where we were due to catch the overnight ferry to Palermo. This was the first firmly-fixed point on the itinerary, as we had booked the crossing in advance. The first thing to do was a big shop, so we took advantage of the giant Leclerc and stocked up on cheese and beer. I also had to buy a roll of sellotape, on account of another little technical matter. The adhesive headlight deflectors, compulsory *sur le continent*, had blown off on the way to Troyes. They naturally don't sell them in France, so I had to improvise by cutting little black rectangles out of a conveniently lugubrious advert for a King Crimson album on the back page of my Record Collector magazine, and attaching them to the headlights with sellotape. I am glad to say that they lasted the whole six weeks. Whether they were legal I don't know, but we didn't once drive in the dark anyway.

In a sweet little town called Aisey-Sur-Seine, we stopped by a little river bridge to consume tea and *mille-feuilles*. Few experiences are more French than entering a village *boulangerie* and purchasing these outrageously indulgent creations of puff-pastry and custard, which invariably spills out as you bite into it and stains your shirt (which has already been stained by the tomato being squeezed out of your baguette).

The camp site in Champagnole was huge and virtually deserted. We were directed to a riverside scenic walk which sadly turned out to encompass a large and malodorous sewage plant, so we instead occupied ourselves with watching another hard-working site owner preparing his pool for the season, before consuming some fresh asparagus we'd bought from a roadside vendor.

Talking about sewage, toilet blocks on campsites are something to be approached with a certain amount of preparation. Some, especially in France, still offer the delightful traditional "flush and run" squatting loos, which can present a challenge if your sense of balance isn't strong. Unless you are experienced in yoga or pilates, you are in danger of tumbling into them as you attempt to maintain your equilibrium. Always take a roll of toilet paper with you. In about fifty percent of loos, there will be none, and a reliable sod's law applies whereby, if you don't take any paper with you, there won't be any, whereas if you do, there will be.

A beautiful drive through the Haute-Savoie and the Jura mountains brought us to the city of Annecy, positioned on the lake of the same name. There were numerous campsites on the lake, and the one we'd chosen was under construction but pleasingly cheap. Our nearest neighbour was of a type that certainly exists under the radar all over Europe: an itinerant Australian who said that he didn't actually live anywhere, but instead simply travelled permanently, living in a converted Transit van and picking up casual work here and there as he went along. I'm not sure if that is an enviable lifestyle or not. Any social contacts he makes can only be very temporary.

Annecy is a beautiful city and thronged with tourists. In a phenomenon that we found replicated almost everywhere we went, as soon as you stepped even a street away from the main tourist area, everyone disappeared and peace reigned. The castle that overlooks Annecy is up a very steep hill, and few people seemed inclined to tackle it, so we spent a good couple of hours virtually alone in this fascinating edifice, which sits on a craggy outcrop overlooking the city and the lake where the tourist paddle steamers ply their trade. Dating from the 13th century, the castle houses the Alpine Lakes Regional Observatory, a detailed exhibition about the preservation of the natural Alpine environment, but as usual, we were on the lookout for other curiosities, which we found in the details of the latrines. "In the sixteenth century," explained the guide book, "the castle benefited from a great interest in toilets, whilst the Court of Louis

XIV in the seventeenth century did not. In the castle, some latrines were intended to seat at least two or three persons." Nice!

Many of the explanatory boards we found around the castle benefited from the "Google Translate" school of interpretation. *"In the architecture of the castles of the Middle Ages, arrow slits appears at the beginning of the twelfth century. They multiply during the thirteenth century in the parts inferiors of bulwarks to allow shaving shootings. By the middle of the fourteenth century, becoming rare in the bottoms of bulwarks, they multiply in their summit thanks to help facilities in the aim and in the shooting which allows the shooting doing downward."* So that's all clear then.

As the campsite restaurant was one of the things under construction, we created a gourmet meal of tinned Heinz spaghetti on toast, something which invariably attracts the attention of neighbours and causes amazement that anyone sane could seriously consume such a plate full of carbohydrates. It's important to have a reserve of tinned food, because almost all the campsites are outside city centres and not within walking distance of restaurants.

In the morning, we discovered that we were next to an attractive marshland nature reserve, so we strolled around amongst the reed beds, being buzzed by the numerous paragliders who were leaping off the top of a nearby mountain, whizzing over the lake and landing with a thump (and remarkably few broken limbs) near where we were parked.

A problem had cropped up which was to bedevil the next couple of weeks, namely rain. Our cunning plan to travel in early summer, hoping to encounter nothing but blissful sunshine, had abjectly failed to come to fruition. As there didn't seem to be much else to do in Annecy in the rain, we decided to carry on, and in no time were passing the romantic-sounding Mont Blanc and Albertville. Sticking to small roads took us via a couple of diversions on account of *routes* being, inexplicably and without warning, *barrée*. An increasing number of statues and placards featuring elephants indicated that we were passing through Hannibal country and, considerably earlier than we had planned, were already traversing the Alps via Mont Cenis.

It was in 218 BC that the military commander Hannibal audaciously led his troops, including cavalry and the infamous African elephants, often referred to as the tanks of their day, over the Alps in order to attempt an ultimately unsuccessful assault on Rome. The Romans had assumed that the mountains formed an unassailable natural barrier, but Hannibal had other ideas. When progress became impossible, they simply stopped for a few days and built themselves improvised roads, which had to be wide and strong enough to support the bulky elephants, who certainly were unused to snow and ice. It was fun to picture this as Polly cautiously negotiated the hairpin bends on the deserted road - nobody else, seemingly, was as mad as Hannibal or us in tackling the route. The picture on the Sat Nav screen looked like a bowl of spaghetti.

In the drizzle, we found ourselves on arguably my favourite campsite of the entire trip, possibly because my inbuilt misanthropy liked the fact that we were the only people there. There weren't even any proprietors to be seen. Incorporated into the mountaintop site was a tiny and very pretty church, featuring an exhibition about the local patron saint, but the facilities included a heated shower block and a games room. Nobody with a larger van, or towing a caravan, would have been able to ascend the road.

As the entire place seemed to be exclusively for us, it got me slightly excited, because it allowed the potential for some indiscreet behaviour, by which I mean nothing more shocking than possibly going to the bathroom without bothering to put on a dressing gown. However, it does lead us to a subject that I have often been questioned about, either directly or by implication, which is: Is it feasible to have sex in a camper van? The answer is, of course, that it's feasible to have sex anywhere. Babies are regularly conceived in tents at Glastonbury Festival, for example. I'm certainly not going to give anything away about our own personal behaviour, but to be frank, I don't think a great deal of it goes on in camper vans, because they tend to bounce around and creak a lot even when all you're doing is climbing in and out of them or walking around in them. They are also normally parked extremely close to other campers, so the likelihood of hanky-panky without drawing anybody's attention is small.

The other rather depressing thing is that a lot of potential neighbours, especially out of season when most of them are pensioners, don't look as if they have had sex for many years. Many of the couples barely even look at each other or speak to each other, far less hold hands or peck each other on the cheek. At any event, my hopes of exclusivity on this delightfully remote campsite were dashed by the arrival of an extremely unfriendly and incommunicative elderly couple who, instead of choosing a spot somewhere else in the huge grounds, decided to draw up immediately adjacent to us. Added to this, a man appeared from the village, demanding to be paid immediately in cash for the overnight stay. He could have been anyone, but we paid him anyway.

While we're on the subject, here's a brief but important diversion about the kind of people that you encounter as you travel around in this strange alternative culture. They're a strange breed, with whom we have little in common, apart from comparing vans, a competition we will always lose on account of Polly's being so small and unpretentious. Some of those vans are just ridiculous. They have huge compartments in the back that contain things like motorbikes. Invariably a couple of sensible bicycles are attached to the rear. These, as far as we can see, seldom get used. Some vans even tow along a little car behind them. Most of them have huge satellite dishes on their roofs, enabling their owners to spend much of the day watching TV rather than showing appreciation for the beautiful places they have chosen to visit.

Incomprehensibly, many campers bring entire menageries of pets along for the holiday with them. Seeing couples disappearing into their vans at night with several large dogs can only lead one to assume they can't have much of a sex life. Or maybe a rather unusual one.

I seldom have a conversation beyond "good morning" with most of these people. Yet you are strangely intimate, because everyone wanders about in their dressing gowns and you share showers and toilets with complete strangers. Washing up can be very dispiriting, because so many of them bring their homely habits on holiday with them, and spend a good half hour doing the dishes after their dinner.

You stand in a row with them all, up to your elbows in soapy bubbles. Germans, in particular, like to bring their entire lifestyle away with them, setting up formal tables (with tablecloths) outside their vans and ritually consuming their habitual breakfast of rolls, cheese and salami as if they'd never left home.

In the drizzly morning, a slightly disturbing technical issue cropped up: Polly's back door wouldn't open. We were stuck inside and the handle moved, but didn't have any effect. I immediately found out how much difficulty that would cause, as I ricked my back attempting to clamber over the front seats in order to escape. With difficulty, I wrenched off a panel in the back door and it was clear to see that the mechanism inside had broken. With a resourcefulness that neither of us realised we had, we repurposed a hairband that Birgit found in her handbag, and improvised a solution that somehow lasted for the next four weeks.

Thus restored, we ascended the *Col de Cenis*, which was no doubt extremely beautiful but was shrouded in fog and the borders of the road were covered with grey-coloured remains of the winter snow. Before we knew it, we passed the nearest thing the Schengen area has to a border post (a wooden hut with a dozy policeman smoking in a small car outside it) and suddenly realized we were in Italy.

5

LIFE AND DEATH

The first day in Italy did not quite pan out as we had hoped. With the help of the guidebook, we had identified what looked like a fascinating place to visit called the Abbey Of San Michele, but finding it was not as straightforward as it seemed. The Sat Nav took us into a small town where all the roads had been blocked off for some kind of carnival, which consisted of a few people huddling from the rain under some gazebos. Once we had manoeuvered our way out of the town, we got stuck going the wrong way along a bypass and had to do a ten-mile detour. The little road that took us to the top of the mountain was winding and dangerous, but the monastery was indeed spectacular and very atmospheric, and with a few fascinating stories to tell as well.

Built on the rocky spur of Mount Pirchiriano, the Monastery is situated at the exact mid-point of a two thousand kilometre pilgrimage route, known as *Via Sancti Michaelis*, which starts at Mont Saint-Michel in Normandy and finishes at Monte Sant'Angelo in Puglia. Over the centuries, the monastery (originally Benedictine but now Rosminian) developed from three chapels built into the rock under what is now the basilica. We entered via the slightly spooky steep stone steps which lead from the entrance to the heavily carved Zodiac Gateway. The rather intimidating staircase goes by the name of *Scalone dei Morti* (Staircase of the Dead). This stems from the bodies of deceased monks that were used to "decorate" the alcoves on both sides of the staircase. Apparently the dead monks' skeletons were still visible until not long ago.

One charming but cautionary legend concerns a lovely peasant girl called Alda, who was allegedly attacked by enemy soldiers when she visited the monastery to offer up prayers against the evils of war. As she tried to escape, she found herself at the top of the tower with no way out. Alda had no choice but to throw herself off the ramparts and into the ravine. She miraculously survived, landing uninjured at the bottom of the cliff. Unfortunately, that made her over-confident and she recklessly undertook a second leap, this time with an admiring audience of villagers in the valley. As miracles never happen twice, Alda found herself splattered on the jagged rocks below.

It was after we had emerged from our tour of the monastery that things started to go astray. I had already been worrying about the exact rules regarding parking, and was relieved not to find a ticket attached the windscreen. Now there was another notice that needed to be interpreted. It appeared to say that the road was one-way only on Sundays, or maybe it was saying it was one-way only *except* on Sundays. We tried to work out whether Sunday would be a more or less busy day than others and decided to watch and see if any cars were going down the hill. Indeed two or three did just that, which seemed to give a clue.

Where we were at the top, there was an unlikely gathering of the local Ford Mustang society, with gleaming, souped-up multi-coloured vehicles being lovingly polished and admired by the crowds. We also spotted a small group of hippies sharing a spliff on a grassy knoll. They disappeared in their rusty old car down the hill, so we thought it would be safe to follow them. It became clear that, probably as a result of what they had inhaled, they were driving at an incredibly slow snail's pace. About half way down, they decided they would like to signal us to overtake, which they did by pulling onto the verge on a blind bend, and beckoning us to pass.

Assuming that it was in fact a one-way street (we hadn't encountered any oncoming traffic), Birgit pulled out to overtake, only to be confronted by another car screaming up the hill at high speed directly towards us. Confronted by us in the middle of the road, the driver slammed on the brakes and skidded directly towards the unguarded precipice. I was absolutely convinced he would plunge over the edge and we would be implicated in a manslaughter case, but by some miracle the wheels halted millimetres from the edge. Putting our hands up to apologise, we slipped through the gap between the two cars and hightailed it down the hill before any unpleasant conversations could take place.

Locating the campsite we had chosen turned out to be a good example of the unreliability of Sat Navs, as we found ourselves in a small hilltop town which had no sign of any camping facilities or any inhabitants. Luckily, we eventually spotted an elegantly-dressed lady, who looked as though she might have been a model in the sixties and spoke perfect English. She explained that the campsite was a couple of miles away and that she often had to redirect baffled tourists.

It was raining heavily when we arrived at the site and turned in to the entrance, to be confronted by closed gates and a notice attached to them saying, "Do not park here, park on the other side of the road". It was slightly too late for this advice and in the ongoing monsoon, it would have been dangerous in the extreme to try and reverse back out onto the main road. The grumpy student on reception greeted me with a right royal telling-off for having disobeyed the sign and was having none of my explanation that the sign was only visible when you reached it.

Reluctantly, she opened the gates and led us up a steep hill on the terraced site. What we didn't know then was that the weather conditions there had been even worse than what we had encountered. This had been the fifth successive day of uninterrupted rain. All the camping slots had turned into quagmires and she entreated us not to park anywhere away from the cinder path. Unfortunately, before I was able to convey this to Birgit, she had spotted what seemed to be a nice pitch and driven into it. Instantly, the wheels started spinning and mud started splashing around in all directions, Polly finally coming to rest at a drunken angle, up to her axles in the mire. Something clearly needed to be done, so I started trying to push, in the hope of helping the wheels get a grip. The only effect of this was for the wheels to completely cake me in mud from head to foot.

What happened next was something that would haunt me for the entire trip, and indeed still wakes me up the middle of the night, shaking. Birgit managed to get Polly moving, but then touched the brake, which had the effect of putting Polly into a gliding motion over which Birgit had no control, as the van drifted majestically through the sludge towards a sheer ten-foot drop. All I could do was watch in despair and assume that Polly would plummet over the edge, which would have smashed her to pieces and inflicted serious injury on Birgit. I almost wished that she had been a couple of feet to the right, which would have meant that she would have crashed into a tree, which would at least have caused slightly less harm.

To my total amazement and immense relief, for the second time in a day, we were saved from disaster as Polly drifted to a halt inches from the edge. We obviously couldn't stay there, but were equally obviously unable to move, as the wheels gained no traction backwards, and forwards was out of the question. The receptionist stood there with her hands on her hips, shaking her head and not offering any advice or help other than saying, "I told you so".

Observing us from nearby was a kind gentleman, who approached me with the information that he had a four-wheel drive Volvo car that might be able to pull us out if we could locate a rope. The campsite owners surprisingly didn't have such an item, but I knocked on the door of a large camper van parked at the bottom of the hill and was able to borrow a rope from its generous owner. With great care and skill, the Swiss Volvo driver gently pulled us to safety, but that wasn't the end of the story. Just as we were thanking him and gasping in relief, a large German camper van rolled up the hill and, before we could stop it, drove straight into the mud lake that we had just vacated. This time, the Volvo would never have had the strength to rescue him, so the poor driver had to wait an hour until the local farmer appeared with his tractor and hauled him out, scraping the side of his van on a tree as he did so.

I can't say we felt very happy at this stage of the trip. In one day, we had got drenched, covered in mud and nearly had two major accidents. The area was called Asti but the mood could hardly have been less *spumante*, as we glumly dined on baked beans on toast and the rain hammered on the roof. Ironically, we had only chosen the site because it had a nice swimming pool.

The following day presented a conundrum, because the ferry we were due to take to Palermo didn't leave Genoa until 11 p.m. From previous experience, we were hesitant about subjecting Polly to the rigours of Genoa traffic, but we had read in a guidebook about a scenic train route through the mountains from a town called Casella to Genoa. As the dire weather didn't offer us much in the way of tourist opportunities, we parked up in Casella and waited with a large and rowdy class of schoolchildren on the scruffy station platform. We half expected a pretty little steam train to chug into the station, but what actually arrived was a noisy, graffiti-covered little two-car diesel train, which rapidly filled up with the schoolchildren and various other commuters. A very strict conductor marched up and down, opening and shutting the doors and selling the expensive tickets as the train grunted and squeaked its way along the winding tracks, stopping every mile or so at deserted stations.

No doubt, on a normal day, the scenery would have been a delight, but as it was, the windows rapidly steamed up and it was impossible to see anything. The journey took almost two hours on very austere and hard, straight-backed seats. The plan had been to have a nice amble round Genoa, but when we arrived there, we realised that not only had the stair-rod rain got even heavier, but also that the terminus was not the central station but some more obscure one, deep in the not particularly attractive suburbs. Therefore, after leaping off for a quick loo visit while the driver reversed the locomotive, we simply remounted the train for the equally dull return journey. This was made even harder for me by a frightening obsession, that had come into my head for no good reason, that Polly would not be safe in the litter-strewn car park where we had left her, so it was a relief to find her intact and sound and not broken into as I had feared. Yes, we had managed to leave both our passports in full view on the dashboard.

Three years previously, we had been semi-traumatized by driving around the outskirts of Genoa, where each road is restricted by double or even triple parked cars, kamikaze scooter riders, terrible pollution and suicidal drivers, often on the wrong side of the road. On that occasion, having taken a wrong turning, we even drove over the Morandi bridge. We knew that this time that would be impossible, on account of its collapse in 2018.

It was on 14 August that year that an unexpected storm hit the city. The bridge, which had been constructed in the 1960s to carry the A10 *autostrada*, and was considered state-of-the-art at the time, became enveloped in a thick mist and, by mid-morning, visibility had become minimal and traffic had to slow right down. Suddenly, and without warning, a 200-metre section of the bridge collapsed, including one of the three towers that held it up. Twenty-seven vehicles plunged into the valley with the remains of the bridge, killing 43 people and making 600 householders who lived beneath it homeless.

We had to drive right into the centre of Genoa and down to the harbour. As we went, we also needed to find a petrol station and some kind of supermarket, both of which were available in abundance, but mysteriously only on the other side of each dual carriageway. As we attempted to negotiate the inexplicable lane system, wild drivers weaved in and out around us, gesticulating and hooting threateningly. Eventually, we found a tiny petrol station that was actually in the shadow of the small remaining part of the Morandi bridge. It was a morose sight, reminiscent, as a doomed structure, of the ruins of Brighton's West Pier.

I was massively cheered up by the friendly lady who served us the diesel. While she did so, she told us her life story and that of her daughter in impeccable English, welcoming us heartily to the city. We had what we thought were detailed instructions on how to find the ferry port, but were severely hindered by the dense traffic, the plethora of roundabouts and the complete and utter lack of any signage. We also gradually realised that the place where you had to check in wasn't the actual port. After several wrong turnings, the Sat Nav plonked us in what seemed to be an unlikely place, a shopping centre with minimal parking facilities and various furtive looking characters hanging around, such as you tend to see at railway stations and ports in most big cities.

I nervously left Birgit in the van and eventually located the place where we had worked out that we would have to exchange our online reservations for physical tickets. It was a huge hall, catering for several different ferry companies and destinations as varied as Corsica, Sardinia, Tunisia, Spain, Sicily, Morocco & Algeria. Of the thirty available windows, only three were staffed and the queues were enormous. Apart from the mild inconvenience of having to stand around for hours, this wasn't really a problem for us, because we had arrived with loads of time to spare. All around, by contrast, were nervous and increasingly angry families and drivers from all over Europe, whose ferries were going to leave much earlier than ours and who were understandably panicking. I began to fear a major riot as minor scuffles and shouting matches started to break out, caused by panicking travellers attempting to jump the queue, but not being able to explain why, in a language that anyone would understand.

Apart from the people behind the windows, who you couldn't actually see, there didn't seem to be any officials around who might have been able to keep some semblance of order. All I could do was look on in amazement at the mass gesticulating, pointing and recriminations that were going on, while occasionally attempting to reassure anybody who spoke a language that I did, such as French, German or English. It was difficult to help the worried families whose ferries were due to leave at any moment, but who were at the back of a slow-moving queue. My phone had no signal, so my anxiety was increased by the thought of Birgit still stuck outside, not knowing where I had gone and potentially threatened by scary attackers. Yes, I do have a vivid imagination.

I felt a tap on my shoulder. It was Birgit, who had suddenly realised that I hadn't taken the passports with me. When we eventually did reach a window, I was utterly convinced that the documentation would be wrong and I would have to go back to the beginning and start again but no, what joy! Having examined the passports (phew), the surly official immediately handed over the required documents and we were able to progress. Giddy with relief, and clearly having lost control of our senses, we treated ourselves to that most evil of rewards (and yes, I feel sullied just thinking about it) a Big Mac. Then, with a lot of backtracking, veering and sudden braking, we made our way to the relative calm of the embarkation pier.

The whole process had taken a good couple of hours, but the terror wasn't quite over. Birgit, normally the world's finest driver, has a hatred of driving on and off ferries, which for some reason we forgot. This was daft, because something like that is pretty much the only thing I can, in fact, efficiently do in a car. As we entered the bowels of the gigantic boat, we realised that, in among the huge juggernauts, we were required to reverse, yes, reverse, down two enormous, steep ramps to get to our allotted place dwarfed between the lorries. I'm telling you, the cold Heineken that we enjoyed in the bar that evening felt very well earned.

---

(6)

ISLAND LIFE

The twenty-eight hour crossing was calm and comfortable. Birgit, normally afflicted by crippling seasickness, merely took a couple of Stugeron and crashed out for ten hours. In the morning, knowing that an entire day on the ferry stretched head of us, we stayed in the cabin and watched a couple of Montalbano episodes before venturing upstairs and spending a few hours playing Bananagrams in the cafeteria, an activity that always attracts attention and enquiries because it looks a bit like Scrabble but isn't. We were surrounded by a modern day phenomenon, namely lorry drivers watching films and TV shows at great volume on their mobile phones in various different languages. It felt like being installed in a mini Tower of Babel, but before we knew it, we were in Sicily.

The sun was setting as we embarked on the terrifying drive to the campsite we had chosen, which lay on the outskirts of Palermo. The map showed that the campsite was off a motorway a few miles out of town, but first we had to get to the motorway. This entailed negotiating narrow streets and having a very sharp learning curve regarding the rules of the road in Palermo. The rules are that there are no rules. This applies in particular to any junction or crossroads, where there is no indication of who may or may not have priority. For a while, we surmised that priority might be to the right, as used to be the case in many European countries, but in fact the only constant seemed to be complete anarchy, as cars were darting across in front of us and behind us and, we assumed, shortly straight into us. Indicators are not used and it's every person for themselves. Once again, we thanked goodness for Polly's small size, as we squeezed between the triple parked cars on the narrow streets, where doors would open with no regard as to whether anybody was about to crash into them. We were grateful that the brakes were working well.

One small thing in our favour was that every other camper van was clearly heading for the same campsite, and most of them were much bigger than us, and having even more difficulty. Eventually, we hit the *autostrada* and were slightly disappointed to find that the campsite was in a litter-strewn and very rundown area. Nevertheless, as we queued to get into it, we were able to take a picture of the sun setting over the sea at the only available angle that was favourable, so that we could post it on Facebook and make it appear idyllic. The reception staff were unfriendly and spent a long time telling each arriving customer about the lengthy list of rules and regulations that had to be followed, but we had arrived, and that was the main thing.

The following morning heralded our big day out in Palermo, and what a wonderful day it turned out to be. For a start, the train station was only a few minutes' walk up the road and, having bought the tickets in a handy tobacco shop (this turned out to be the norm for purchasing any transport documents, good thing we asked), we were whisked into the centre of the city by a very swish, silent and brand new train.

The day was spent in a semi-religious world, as we darted in and out of a lengthy series of churches, cathedrals and oratories. The difference between them was not immediately clear, but we were to find out more details about that later in the day. All the buildings were uniformly ornate, decorated by frescoes and full of unique artefacts. In the cathedral, it was possible to climb up and walk around the roof, which was not good for my vertigo, especially when I dropped my pen, which clattered down onto the crowds in the square below. The cathedral was expensive to get into, but admission to the rest of the churches varied dramatically. Some were entirely free, others had a shy-looking person on the door, collecting a "suggested donation" of a couple of euros, while others were unaccountably expensive, twenty euros or more. These we didn't enter, on the basis that once you've seen one bloodthirsty picture of Christ on the cross or a suffering virgin, you've seen them all. Not entirely true, but you get the drift.

As we exited the cathedral, we had a minor disagreement on the subject of ice cream. Obviously, an ice cream is compulsory every single day in Italy or Sicily, but Birgit was about to disappear into a *gelateria* directly outside the cathedral. I tried to explain that the prices here would obviously be a rip-off, as we were in the centre of the tourist area. In my opinion, it would be better to go down a side street in a quieter area, where we would be bound to find better quality, artisan ice cream. Birgit was having none of it and, to my subsequent embarrassment, we found that this was, in fact, the cheapest and most delicious ice cream in Palermo.

In the sunshine, yes, sunshine, the entire city had an aura

of mild yellowness, which somehow induced a good mood as we wandered the alleys. It was important to take a good look at each doorway, because often even the most insignificant-looking entrances would lead into magnificent churches and ornate palazzos. As we were wandering around, we noticed a sudden increase in street vendors selling long-stemmed roses and large crowds of people disappearing into a particular oratory. Inside, a service was taking place, and the building was crammed with people brandishing the flowers. A quick pidgin Italian enquiry elicited the fact that this was May 22, the feast of Saint Rita (of course, how could we have forgotten?). This was her particular church, and the atmosphere was so startlingly mystical that both of us were almost overcome to experience such a calm and spiritual gathering in the middle of such a busy city.

Saint Rita, known as the Patron Saint Of The Impossible, had quite a life. The day after she was baptised, a swarm of white bees appeared and went into her mouth without stinging her. This convinced her family that her life was to be devoted to God. It didn't work out that way, though. She was subjected to an arranged marriage to a man called Paolo Mancini, who turned out to be cruel and violent. Rita gave birth to her first child at the age of twelve and her husband often abused her, both verbally and physically, and cheated on her with other women.

Paolo Mancini was killed during a feud with the Chiqui family. This created a desire in Rita's two sons, Giovanni Antonio and Paulo Maria, to avenge his murder. Rita, wanting her sons to avoid the sin of murder, prayed to God for them to be stopped, and shortly afterwards, they both contracted dysentery and died. At the age of 36, Rita entered a monastery, where she asked to be allowed to suffer like Christ had. Immediately, a scar appeared on her forehead, which did not heal, causing her pain for the rest of her life.

As for the rose ceremony, it's the culmination of a pilgrimage inspired by Rita herself. Apparently, Saint Rita, at the end of her life, had been bedridden for four years with tuberculosis. She was visited by a relative, who asked if Rita wanted something from her home. Rita requested a rose from her own garden, even though it was the middle of winter. Nevertheless, the relative amazingly found a lovely fresh pink rose in Rita's orchard. Nowadays, at the ceremony we witnessed, people bring the roses, which are blessed by priests and then preserved in the homes of the faithful, to protect them from evil. We, unfortunately, failed to purchase a rose for Polly, which might have helped to avoid some of the evils which were coming down the line at us.

Well, it's all a load of bollocks, of course, but who can

resist a good story and an emotional ceremony? We emerged from the church quite moved.

At the centre of Palermo lies a square with buildings at all four corners. This is known, unsurprisingly, as Quattro Canti. Just around the corner, we found a little piazza where something mysterious was going on in the middle. A lorry was winching a large square object onto the cobbles, guarded by several police vans and a number of officers. A small crowd had gathered to watch what was going on, so we joined them. Over the course of the next half an hour, the wrapping was gradually removed from the box, which turned out to be a glass display case. Inside the case was something which we initially thought was a bizarre piece of modern art, but closer examination revealed to be the tangled remains of a destroyed car.

Gradually, it became clear that the next day, May 23, was the anniversary of the assassination of Judge Giovanni Falcone by the Mafia on May 23, 1992. This exhibit is displayed each year on that day, not only in memory of Falcone, but also as a warning for the future, as a nearby museum confirms that the Mafia is still influential in Sicily.

Falcone's murder was carried out with a car bomb filled with more than half a ton of explosives. Surely one of the most courageous Europeans of the twentieth century, Falcone had fought the Mafia throughout his life. It was inevitable that his efforts would cost him his life and, in the end, they did. Born in a poor area of Palermo, Falcone observed the horrors carried out by the Mafia from a young age and dedicated his life as a judge to challenging corruption in Sicily. Inspired by the assassinations of Judge Cesare Terranova and head of police Boris Giuliano, who were prosecutors tackling the Mafia's drug trafficking, Falcone concentrated his mind on anti-Mafia investigations, but this had a dramatic effect on his way of life. Everywhere he went, he had to be escorted by a fleet of armoured vehicles. His office was in a rocket-proof bunker in the centre of Palermo.

Falcone led the prosecution for the so-called Maxi trial, which lasted for nearly two years in 1986 and 1987 and resulted in the conviction of 360 Mafiosi involved in the shipment of heroin from Sicily to New York. But Falcone knew that he was signing his own death warrant.

Angry and frustrated by the inroads Falcone was making into their criminal activities, the Mafiosi were determined to rid themselves of him. The eventual attack took place on the highway from Palermo Airport to the city centre, which was a route that Falcone regularly took. The bombs were detonated by remote control, blowing up a portion of the highway with accurate enough timing to kill Falcone, along with his wife, and three members of his security guard.

So it was by pure chance that we were in Palermo on such an important anniversary in its history. The influence of the Mafia has very much diminished in recent years, partly because of stricter prison régimes for arrested members. This improvement can be seen in the shop windows of Palermo, many displaying a sticker with the word *Addiopizzo* - Goodbye To Extortion. This indicates the decline in willingness to pay protection money, but the reality is that the Mafia, while being on the retreat, is far from dead.

A sunny day in Italy or Sicily is synonymous with Aperol Spritz, the highly addictive and slightly bitter cocktail made up of Campari, fizzy water and prosecco, so we proceeded to sit outside a cafe and consume one, along with an item which was to become an almost daily delight, namely *Arancine*. Basically, it's a blob of risotto rolled into a ball and fried in breadcrumbs. They often contain cheese and ham but we tended to go for the spinach ones. These delicacies are actually probably terribly bad for you, as they are deep-fried and dripping with grease.

Another prominent person of whom traces are to be found everywhere in Palermo was the military leader Giuseppe Garibaldi. Travellers in modern-day Italy often forget that it has existed as a country for a relatively short time. The *Risorgimento*, as Italian Unification was called, was only completed as late as 1861. The Congress Of Vienna in 1815 had left Italy in tatters and largely governed by Austria, with Piedmont, Nice, Genoa and Savoy in the hands of the Kingdom of Sardinia, on the border of France. The Kingdom of Sardinia consisted of the region called Piedmont in the north west of Italy, plus the island of Sardinia. Sicily and the southern half of the peninsula were known as the Kingdom of the Two Sicilies. Other small states included Modena, Tuscany and Parma, which were monarchies, governed by family members of the Habsburgs of Austria.

General Garibaldi was a committed advocate of Italian unity and his greatest achievement came with the conquest of Sicily and Naples in 1860. Sailing from Genoa on May 6 with an army of 1,000 men, he soon reached Marsala in Sicily and pronounced himself dictator. Finding a high level of support on the island, he was able to capture Palermo before the end of May. By July, he had conquered the rest of Sicily, before crossing over the Strait Of Messina and landing in Calabria. By September 1860, he had taken Naples, and proceeded to proclaim himself "Dictator Of The Two Sicilies". But he soon handed control to King Victor Emmanuel, who was declared as the king of a united Italy in 1861.

Astonishingly, for someone proudly calling himself a

dictator and a nationalist, Garibaldi thought of himself as a socialist. As a result of his war experiences, he also became a pacifist, and was a strong advocate for workers' rights and female emancipation. He is viewed as having been ahead of his time in believing in supporting racial equality and the abolition of capital punishment.

In a city like Palermo, even getting lost is fun, and we almost wilfully did so, darting down small streets just to see where they would lead. This was extra rewarding when we found ourselves in a cavernous and impressive oratory called Oratorio del Rosario. Here, we were approached by two young teenage volunteer guides called Dario and Antonino, who seemed very impressed that we had come all the way from the UK to visit them. They lived in Monreale, where we were planning to head the next day, so as well as filling us in on the details of that town, they also explained exactly what an oratory is. It seemed to us pretty much like a normal church, and the difference is subtle. An oratory is a place of prayer, but technically it means a building other than a church, set up by the clergy for prayer and the celebration of mass. Originally, they were chapels built over the tombs of martyrs where the faithful went to pray, and presented a place of worship for people in remote areas where no churches were available.

We found it quite inspiring that teenagers in this largely horrible modern world could be so polite, kind, welcoming and religious in a tolerant and understated way. The only problem was that, even though we were semi-whispering in an appropriately ecclesiastical manner, something seemed to be preventing me from hearing properly. This was the beginning of a minor but slightly upsetting medical problem that was to continue for several days.

My father went deaf at a very young age and I have spent much of my life pressed up against raging loudspeakers blasting out rock music, so I've always had an assumption that one day I, too, would be unable to hear. Lo, here in Palermo, it all seemed to be kicking off. From my left ear I could hear absolutely nothing, a fact that I gradually realised was putting me in physical danger, as I couldn't hear cars approaching. Also, conversations were beginning to occur which went like this:

Birgit: "???!!!????!!"

Me: "What?"

Birgit: "???!!!????!!"

Me: "What?"

Birgit: "Are you going deaf?"

Me: "Deaf? Of course not, whatever do you mean?"

Reluctant to admit that it was really happening, I had to

acknowledge that something was going wrong and that I really needed to do something about it. Excessive yawning, wiggling of finger in ear and shaking of head were having no effect.

Regardless of any of this, it was time for dinner. As we had wandered the streets, we had found a few areas consisting almost entirely of restaurants. I'm sure all tourists have done this at one time or another. You pick a couple of restaurants you think might be all right and plan to come back later on, but by the time later on comes, you can't remember where your chosen restaurant was. En route, one of the many waiters patrolling outside and beckoning us into their establishments had given us a card and promised us that, if we brought it back, we would get a discount and a free carafe of wine. To help in the decision-making process, we looked up the address and returned to him, hoping he hadn't forgotten his promise.

All was well. The "nothing special" meal turned out to be nice and cheap and the wine was indeed free. Would this be something that every Sicilian restaurant would offer? We hoped so. Neither of us know anything about wine, as we normally don't drink it, but when it's free ... It tasted perfectly all right to us and we slurped it down before heading back to the station and the empty luxury train.

In the morning, I decided I needed to wash my hair, but the sponge bag revealed that I must have left my bottle of Head And Shoulders in a shower cubicle at one of our preceding stops. How was I to go about purchasing some anti-dandruff shampoo? Considering how much I pontificate about the importance of learning foreign languages, it was remiss of me to fail to brush up on my Italian before this trip. It was a mixture of being too busy and too lazy. I'm fine when it comes to cheerily greeting people and ordering simple things in restaurants and bars, in fact I make it a point of honour to scatter round *prego, pronto, bongiorno* and *ciao*, but this was beyond my capabilities. In the end, I simply marched into the camp shop, pointed at my head and declared "*Piccolo blanco thingies*". It worked like a charm. The Italian for dandruff, as everyone surely knows, is *forfola*.

Armed with this expensive but hopefully effective toiletry, I headed for the shower block. If you are going from campsite to campsite, you have no way of knowing what will confront you in the ablution stakes. You can be lucky and find recently refurbished shower blocks which can run to central heating and piped music, as well as that shower essential: a small anteroom where you can plonk your shoes and clothes while you venture beyond into the cubicle. You can also be unlucky and find a freezing, filthy and, crucially, tiny box, where there is no facility at all for protecting your garments, towel and footwear, which will get drenched, unless you are brave enough to leave them unguarded outside. In that case, you will also have to wander around the facilities naked, which can sometimes be an issue, as many of the shower blocks are unisex.

Once inside the shower, you can be confronted by anything from ice-cold, to lukewarm, to scalding hot water, coming out either in a whoosh or a dribble. More often than not, you will have had to purchase a token from reception and not have any idea when it will run out and leave you stranded, covered in lather. But that's the name of the game and what the heck, you're on holiday, so you might as well just take whatever you're given.

It was the day of the European elections but we were surprised to find there was absolutely no hint of anything political going on at all, either in France, Italy or Sicily, all of which I had thought were extremely politically diverse and passionate countries. We saw no sign of any rallies, polling stations or even posters, and were forced to the conclusion that politics, along with everything else, has transferred itself online.

---(7)---

DEAF SCHOOL

Our next stop was to be the hugely impressive religious complex of Monreale, not too far out of Palermo. Reaching it wasn't easy, because the main car park was underground and Polly's roof was too high to fit under the barrier. We therefore had to park precariously on the edge of a busy road out of town and dodge the traffic as we walked back down the hill. But it was worth it.

The huge Norman *duomo*, dating from the twelfth century, is famous for its mosaics. There are more than 6,000 square metres of gleaming gold mosaics, completely covering the upper part of the cathedral's interior. It's spectacular and inspiring. We also bought an extra ticket for a spot of *déjà vu*, namely climbing up to the panoramic roof terrace, just as we had done in Palermo's *duomo* the day before. This ascent was rather more hurried, as they were about to close the entire attraction for a lengthy lunch break, something we had to get used to (and plan for) throughout the entire trip.

The itinerary we had planned was to lead us all the way around the island of Sicily, which was much bigger than we had imagined. It was due to end up at Villa San Giovanni, where we would be able to cross the straits over to Messina in Italy for the long drive back up North. Places we had spotted on the map included Castellammare and Scopello but in the end we decided to bypass both of these, because visiting them would have entailed us backtracking afterwards. Instead, we headed to San Vito Lo Capo, which appeared to be a seaside resort at the very northernmost tip of a cape in the North West of the island. A large chunk of the journey was done on a pleasingly quiet, if rather potholed, *autostrada*, which had the advantage that its toll booths were out of service and therefore didn't charge us.

As we moved onto smaller roads, we noticed something quite unexpected. Always on the lookout for nice lay-bys to stop in for a picnic, we discovered that this was impossible. The reason was that each lay-by was piled high with dumped rubbish. By this I don't mean the normal fly-tipping that you see by many UK roads, consisting of sofas and fridges and such, and I also don't mean the kind of fast food detritus that you'll find scattered at the edge of UK roads. These lay-bys were proper little landfill sites, consisting of not just a few, but piles up to six feet high of bin liners, full of household rubbish, most of which had been attacked by dogs, foxes, rats or other animals. The contents, consisting of rotten vegetables, soiled nappies, broken bottles, jagged cans etc, spilled out onto the tarmac. Frankly, we had never seen anything like it, and it made any chance of stopping to enjoy the countryside out of the question.

Later, I tried Googling to find out what the reason for this horror might be. We wondered whether the bin operatives might have been on strike, or whether it was connected in some way with the Mafia, or whether perhaps high prices were charged for collecting refuse, but I have failed to find any explanation for it. As we continued driving around for the next week, this was a regular pattern, except when we approached tourist areas, at which point everything miraculously became sparklingly clean.

We arrived at the San Vito campsite and were once again confronted with a beautiful swimming pool, whose surface was dappled by the incessant raindrops. By now, I was getting seriously concerned about my ear problem. Birgit reassured me that it was almost certainly just excessive wax, but being prone to ultra hypochondria and extreme over-dramatisation, I was convinced that I was about to go permanently deaf.

"Well, you'll have to go to the doctor then, won't you?"

"I suppose so, but what if there isn't a doctor?"

"Of course there'll be a doctor. What do you think all the people who live here do when they're unwell?"

I approached the gentleman on campsite reception and the use of sign language and grimacing elicited the fact that the doctor's surgery was on the other side of town, about a two-mile walk. The receptionist helpfully drew the rather long and complicated route in biro on a tourist map he gave me. Cocking my only functioning ear towards him, I made further enquiries.

"When are they open?"

"They're always open."

"Always? All day and all night?"

"Yes, it's an emergency doctor. You have an emergency, yes?"

Obviously my gurning had been suitably convincing.

"Yes, it's an emergency," I agreed.

It was mid-afternoon, so I thought I might as well head straight off. The rain had ceased and a glimpse of sunshine was peeking through, so Birgit was determined to brave the swimming pool come what may. I headed off along the seafront and became increasingly cheered by the fact that it seemed a really nice place, with a huge sandy beach and lots of little bars and restaurants, almost all of them closed, as it was pre-season. The route took me through the centre of town and out to a suburb on the other side, where I located the surgery. It was shuttered and both of its doors were firmly locked. Outside in the street stood a rickety ambulance, which was plugged into a lamp post, presumably being charged up. Persistent knocking brought a green-suited paramedic to the door. He explained that, far from being permanently open, the emergency surgery only functioned for an hour a day, from 8 p.m. to 9 p.m.

As it was only 5 o'clock, I texted Birgit who, refreshed from her swim, agreed to come into town to meet me. I wandered the streets and filled time by going into the central church. Entering a church was a compulsory element of every place we visited. We met in a seafront bar, where I took a bit of a risk.

"Do you think I dare have an Aperol Spritz?"

"What do you mean, do you dare?"

"Well, I'm about to go to see the doctor."

"So what?"

"Aperol Spritz is alcohol."

"Don't be so daft. There's no law against drinking alcohol, is there?"

Thus it was that I was probably smelling mildly of Campari as we returned to the dingy waiting room, which was now open. Behind us in the queue were a worried young couple with a hysterical baby, and also an elderly man who was coughing rather violently. This made me feel slightly guilty and put my deafness into perspective, so I gestured to both of them to go in before me, which they accepted with grateful looks in their eyes.

The doctor turned out to be a rather attractive young lady. She spoke perfect English, so I was able to explain my predicament. She opened a drawer and took out one of those trumpet-like implements that doctors use to look in ears.

"Right ear, please."

"No, the problem's in my left ear."

"Right ear, please."

"If you say so."

She rammed the trumpet into my right ear and immediately pronounced:

"This ear is full of wax."

"No, it's the other ..."

"Now I will look in the other ear."

In went to the trumpet. The doctor let out a gasp and recoiled.

"This is bad, this is very, very bad."

My stomach turned a somersault. Oh God, I was going to have to be hospitalized. The holiday would have to be cancelled. I would have to be flown home at vast expense. The insurance would never cover it. I would never hear my granddaughter speak again.

"You have a very bad infection. I will prescribe you antibiotics and refer you to the hospital."

"The hospital?"

"Yes, the hospital in Scopello. It is one hour by car. But first you must take antibiotics for a week."

This was a real shocker and for a moment, I was speechless. It meant the end of our holiday in Sicily.

"What will they do at the hospital?"

"They will clear the wax out of your ears, but first you must take some drops to soften the wax in your right ear and you must take the antibiotics to clear the infection in your left ear."

The message was clear and I felt grateful that the doctor was clearly so efficient and straightforward. It only remained for her to inform me that the pharmacies wouldn't be open again until the next day. Birgit and I trudged home feeling pretty doomish, but by the time we got back to Polly, we had made a decision. I could just as well get my ears syringed when we got back to the UK, and for the time being, if I was going to be deaf, I was going to be deaf. I was convinced that the five-day course of antibiotics was not working because I initially couldn't discern any improvement. But suddenly, precisely at the end of day five, the infected ear magically cleared and everything returned to normal. That is, in fact, the end of the story, and I promise not to mention it again.

The morning brought another abject example of my lack of Italian language skills. In the pharmacy, all was okay. I merely shoved the prescription at the pharmacist. It was in the post office, where I had to go to pay for the treatment, that things kicked off, with the staff shouting and gesticulating at my inability to understand that I should have written down my name and address in the box on the paper, rather than placing a signature there. Still, as the entire procedure (consultation and medication) came to a grand total of nineteen euros, I wasn't going to argue.

The plan we had made to visit various scenic seaside spots and lounge on beaches was being well and truly stymied by the weather, which remained chilly and very rainy, so we decided to just meander on and visit a few places recommended in the guidebook. The first of these was a quite remarkable mediaeval hilltop town called Erice. We parked at the bottom of the hill in Trapani and took the long cable car journey to the top. The little cabin bounced alarmingly in the wind as we were tossed around. As it felt actually quite romantic, I toyed with the idea of stealing a little kiss until Birgit pointed out that there was a CCTV camera focused on us. Bloody hell, you can't get any privacy anywhere.

In Erice, prior to embarking on an attempt on the world record for the greatest number of churches to be entered in one afternoon, we first breathlessly ascended the 108 steps of King Frederick's Tower, from where we could see right out to the pretty Egadi Islands. The Royal Church featured a lavish stuccoed ceiling which, rather worryingly, had collapsed and been reinstated on several occasions. In San Salvatore's Monastery, we admired the ancient water cisterns and the bread ovens used by the nuns in the 13th century. Oddly, when they died, the nuns were placed in the crypt for dessication, prior to being removed and placed in an ossuary, in order to make space for the next lot of ex-nuns. Erice, once known as the City of a Hundred Churches, now has just seventeen, some of them only recently restored. After visiting about five, we could cope with no more frescoes, relics, treasures, naves, apses, altars and statues and retreated from the freezing elements into a café serving the traditional sweets made by the nuns in their cloisters.

We stuttered on to a dull campsite near Marsala and prepared to spend the evening completing a half-finished episode of Inspector Montalbano. "Oh shit!" I heard a cry, and looked up to see Birgit holding the DVD player in one hand and a severed cable with the plug in the other. Somehow or other, the cable had snapped and, as the machine only worked on mains electricity, that would surely spell the end of our private cinema entertainment for the entire holiday. We would never find out whether Salvo solved the case although, to be fair, I'm sure he did, because he always solves every case. The writer Andrea Camilleri died just a few months later and his obituaries revealed that he wrote every story to a strict format, so an unsolved case would have been unthinkable. From now on, evening entertainment would return to crossword puzzles and Kindles.

The delicious spicy taste conjured up by the name Marsala was not to be emulated by dinner that evening, which was, once again, Heinz spaghetti on toast, this time with a fried egg on top and brown sauce. No doubt we would have got the traditional funny looks from fellow campers, but they were all firmly shut inside their vehicles, away from the elements.

My diary entry for the next day had a depressing start: "Cold, wet, windy, deaf, no DVD, Birgit's phone out of data, not much of a day." Yes indeed, first world problems all of them. Getting set up with some more data in order to communicate with family at home was quite a rigmarole. The trip hit a dismal low as we lunched in the scruffy car park of a closed supermarket. Any thoughts of tourist activity had to be banished.

As we drove through a particularly unexciting village, the eagle-eyed Birgit suddenly called out:

"Look, an electrical shop!"

"There's no point in stopping," I replied. "Not only is it lunchtime, when everything shuts, but it's also a Sunday."

I think, in truth, I just didn't fancy getting drenched on a doubtless doomed mission to find an obscure electrical cable.

"Surely it's worth having a look," said Birgit, as she drove around a roundabout and headed back towards the town centre. The shop was dark but its door was open and I ventured in. In the shadows at the back, stocking up some shelves, was a Chinese lady who seemed to speak neither Italian nor English. She smiled when I pointed at the severed cable, disappeared behind some shelves and returned with several shrink-wrapped items, which she proceeded to open and link together. Eventually, she had created something that did indeed look like a cable connected to a British style three-pin plug and I felt my hopes rising. She plugged the DVD player into the mains and, to my amazement, the screen flickered into light. I almost, but not quite, gave her a little hug. At least the damp evenings would continue to offer some visual entertainment, I thought, as I gratefully handed over the 28 euros that she scribbled on a piece of paper.

We were en route to checking out the Valley Of The Temples, one of Sicily's premier historical sites. With excellent timing, the rains ceased for a couple of hours exactly at the time we arrived, having negotiated a complicated bypass that brought us to the slightly primitive car park. Here, some taxi drivers were plying their trade, offering to take customers to the main entrance, with the option of walking back along the valley and eventually returning to the car park. At five euros, this seemed an excellent deal, especially as the clouds were already beginning to reassemble on the horizon.

At the entrance, I gave my traditional disapproving look to the young official as he assured me that there was no discount for pensioners, even though there was a long list of other categories of people who qualified for reduced admission.

The valley (more of an escarpment, really) is an amazing example of Greek art and architecture, and is one of the main attractions of Sicily, as well as a national monument of Italy. The area was designated a UNESCO World Heritage Site in 1997. At 1,300 hectares, the complex is the largest archaeological site in the world. It contains seven temples, all Doric in style and dating from the fifth century BC, and in varying states of repair.

We wondered why Greek architecture like this was to be found in Sicily, and research showed that in the eighth and seventh centuries BC, the Greeks had been on a colonization drive, establishing settlements in Sicily and the southern part of the Italian peninsula. The Romans called the area encompassing Sicily and the lower part of Italy's boot "Greater Greece", because it was so substantially populated by Greeks.

The Valley Of The Temples is divided into two zones, the Eastern and the Western. Received wisdom is that the Eastern Zone is the more impressive, because more of the buildings are nearly intact. Here we found the Temple Of Castor and Pollux, the twin brothers of legend, born from the union of Jupiter and the Queen of Sparta. It only has four columns left but it is the main symbol of Agrigento. The Temple Of Concordia, also built in the fifth century, is particularly well-preserved. The temple of Heracles is the oldest one but, attacked over the years by war and natural disasters, now has only eight columns left. At the Temple Of Juno, we were able to examine the traces of the fire - amazingly, still visible on the walls - that was set by the Carthaginians.

On balance, we actually preferred the cheerful chaos of the Western Zone, which contains the remains of collapsed temples. Scattered around on the ground lie gigantic recumbent stone figures, including an eight metre-long *telamone*, a stone male figure who, in his time, would have formed one of the columns holding up the temple's roof. We spent about half an hour in this spookily atmospheric stone jungle, stalking a young couple who were both so staggeringly attractive that we assumed they must be film stars.

One building that is intact is a much more modern one, positioned in the centre of the park. This is the Villa Aurea, which was the home, between 1921 and 1932, of Sir Alexander Hardcastle, a wealthy nobleman who had been a captain in the British army. He bought the estate at the end of the nineteenth century, and over this period, devoted his wealth and archaeological skills to extensive excavation and research work. The gardens of the villa are now open to the public and form the centrepiece of the valley, but there was a sad coda to his career. The Wall Street Crash of 1929 left the poor man destitute and he was forced to sell the estate to the Italian government. He fell into a deep depression and was committed to an asylum in Agrigento, before dying in 1933.

Having successfully walked the entire length of the valley without the heavens opening, we checked into a campsite on the edge of Agrigento town and found a quiet spot. The evening did not go well.

8

GAS BOARD

Before setting off from home, I'd been very efficient and stocked up with two full gas canisters, which should have been easily enough to last us the six weeks. It was therefore slightly unnerving to find that the first one was empty after less than two weeks. It sputtered out just as the tomato soup we were warming up started to bubble. Still not particularly bothered, I crouched down in the mud with my spanner, detached the canister and, with some difficulty, manoeuvered the second one into place and connected it.

Well, I hadn't been bothered, but I should have been. This second canister gave up the ghost after just a couple of minutes, which wasn't long enough even to bring the soup back to the boil. Now we really were in trouble. What could be the explanation?

I had noticed a slight smell of gas a few times and therefore assumed that there must be some kind of a leak, which would explain the sudden lack of gas. But, until the morning, there was nothing else we could do, and I was reasonably confident that surely, somehow, we'd be able to stock up again. After all, thousands of tourists must constantly pass through this area and encounter similar needs. We spent the evening Googling camping gas suppliers in the area and adjourned to bed, where we were glad that at least we would at least be able to enjoy a DVD. Wrong! When I switched it on, I discovered that, although the screen light came on, there was no actual picture. So that was the definitive end of that.

In the morning, I walked down to reception in order to buy a shower token, but was ignored by the receptionist, who was more interested in using a mobile phone to take some photographs of something that was going on by the exit. A very old Swedish gentleman and his wife had managed to crash their huge caravan into the barrier which went up and down to control traffic flow in and out of the campsite. They had got their vehicle stuck on the large box containing the electric mechanism and were desperately trying to free themselves. A few other people joined in and eventually they were disentangled, but not without inflicting a certain amount of damage on the equipment. The old man got back into his Volvo and appeared to be about to drive off, when the campsite owner came hurtling down the hill, breathing through flamed nostrils like a charging bull. He dragged the unfortunate pensioner from his car and proceeded to hold him up against the wall by his neck, shouting hysterical saliva-flecked threats into his face. At this stage, sensing an imminent murder, the receptionist at last stirred herself into action and went over to try and make peace. It was then that I decided not to bother with a shower after all, and we sneaked out past the gathering crowds of onlookers.

While Googling, we had been encouraged by seeing a detailed website from a particular shop, quite nearby, which set out the vast range of camping gas products they stocked. When we eventually found it, however, at the end of a potholed lane, it turned out to be a pet food supplier. The people there were extremely unfriendly and unhelpful to the point of almost being obstructive. I persisted and eventually, with great reluctance, they scribbled down an address for someone who might be able to help. We were on the edge of Agrigento at the time and the traffic chaos was even worse than what we had encountered elsewhere in Sicily, so it was with great relief that we eventually found the shop, Tutti Gas.

Amazingly, the proprietor, Marco, was a Sicilian, but had been born in Vauxhall Bridge Road in London and spoke charming English with a Cockney accent. I immediately felt better, as he braved the passing juggernauts and came out to have a look. Sadly, however, he was unable to help, as he did not have the right fittings to be able to supply us with any gas. The problem, it was clear, was that any canisters he had didn't have UK fittings, and he didn't have any fittings to fill up the empty canisters we had. Does that make sense?

This reminded me of a previous trip we had taken to Slovenia. On that occasion, we had had to take a seventy mile detour to Ljubljana to go to a specialist gas site, where some very friendly fitters had refilled our canisters and plied us with fresh cherries as they worked. So I knew it was possible, we just had to find someone who was able to do it.

Marco professed with great confidence that he had a friend who would be our saviour. Following his instructions, we found ourselves, surreally, right back at the campsite where we had first started. Having checked that there were no dead bodies of Swedish pensioners on the ground, we sought out the shop, which turned out to be directly opposite. It was no wonder we hadn't spotted it, as it was a fishing tackle shop and didn't even have a sign outside it. I waited for nearly half an hour while the proprietor dealt with the queue of anglers in front of me, choosing their flies and floats. He immediately made it clear he was also unable to help, but he made a few phone calls and eventually wrote down an address on a piece of paper.

"Does that say Marco?"

"Sì."

"At Tutti Gas?"

"Sì."

"Uh-oh, already been there ..."

After some more calls, he gave us the address of a gas wholesaler in the next town. We drove there to an utterly desolate industrial estate, where we encountered our most unhelpful person yet, who merely scornfully pooh-poohed our canisters, waved his finger, shook his head repeatedly and shouted, "No, no, no, no, no." Nearby, one of his colleagues, seeing our sorrow, took pity on us, beckoned us to follow him and leapt into his car. We proceeded at great speed down dangerous roads to yet another bleak and dark industrial estate (remember all this was going on in the rain), where he left us by the firmly locked gate and sped off. It all felt quite frightening.

"Are we in danger?"

"What do you mean?"

"Maybe this place is run by the Mafia?"

"Well, ring the bell and we'll find out."

I pressed the bell and instantly knew from the faces of the staff that the response would be the same: firmly wagging fingers, shaking heads and "No, no, no, no, no". There was nothing for it but cold meals for us from now on, and we consoled ourselves with the acceptance that, in the great scheme of things, it didn't really matter.

Having finally accepted our fate, we set off on what turned out to be a very unattractive route to a seaside village called Punta Bracasetto. We were in an area dominated by fruit and vegetable cultivation and frequently had to give way to gigantic lorries filled with these items. It might sound relatively pleasant but boy, would that be wrong. The fruit and veg, you see, was all being grown under enormous polytunnels, which completely dominated the entire landscape for mile after mile. For anyone unfamiliar with polytunnels, they consist of a semicircular length of scaffolding, covered with huge expanses of plastic sheeting. The problem here, apart from the extreme ugliness, was that the farmers clearly had a policy of abandoning the polytunnels as they fell into disrepair. This seemed to be very common, as we were in an exposed coastal area, presumably prone to high winds. Instead of replacing the plastic sheeting, the farmers merely built new rows of polytunnels adjacent to the abandoned ones.

What became of the plastic? Why, of course, most of it was blown over the fields, onto the roads and eventually, inevitably, into the sea. We are well aware of the environmental issues caused by plastic bottles, but this was a similar problem on a much vaster scale. Frankly, we were disgusted and repelled by the whole thing and in a pretty bad mood when we arrived at the hyperbolically titled Camping Luminosa, which was one of a series of adjacent seafront sites.

We were told that we could park up anywhere, so duly drove right down to the seafront and took a scenic slot looking straight out over the beach. Behind us were upwards of thirty vintage Citroen 2CVs that were on a round the island rally. We were to bump into them several more times as we travelled. I was not best pleased when, returning to reception in order to tell them where we had decided to park, I was informed that seafront slots entailed an extra charge of five euros, something they had failed to mention previously. They also informed us that the pizza service, as advertised in the office, was not actually available. Another cold supper coming up, then. I took revenge by reversing the van into such a position that no one could get in front of us and we still had an uninterrupted sea view.

We sat on the windy beach for a while, and then I got into conversation with the French lady who was parked next to us. In her van was a rather pretty cat, so I tried to talk to her about how it was to travel with your pet. As we know, dogs are common in camper vans, but this was the first time I had seen a feline companion. What she told me took my breath away. This wasn't their pet from home. It was a cat that they had found a few days before on another campsite on the other side of the island, and simply decided to take with them. She saw absolutely nothing odd or potentially cruel about this behaviour, so I feigned having an important appointment and terminated the conversation.

Just as we were about to leave the next morning, we got into a brief conversation with Stan from Doncaster, who was the elderly husband of the mother of the campsite proprietor. Stan assured us confidently that the next town had a shop owned by somebody called Toni, who would definitely be able to help us with the gas. Having absolutely no hope that this would possibly be true, we nonetheless drove to the town and located the shop. Running the place were one person who was a deaf mute and another who was senile, but luckily Toni arrived eventually. Toni took one look at our canisters, announced (via a very helpful Google

Translate app on his phone, which he held up to my face) that if we left them with him, he would deliver them back to the campsite at five o'clock, and indeed that is exactly what he did. He also charged us just fourteen euros for the entire job (filling the canisters at home had cost thirty quid each). Now all we could do was hope that there wasn't an actual leak and that they might keep us going till the end of the holiday.

There is a coda to this, which I'll fast forward to now, lest I forget. The canisters actually did last us until we got home, and indeed much longer (three weekend music festivals, in fact, before even the first one was empty). Clearly, Toni had filled them up properly, unlike our local camp shop. We had the system checked over and no leaks were found. Clearly, we had been sold duff, empty canisters.

While Toni was sorting the gas, we had a day to fill. What better to do than go in search of Inspector Montalbano? But there was a problem. The town of Vigàta, where the stories are set, is fictional. Enquiries elicited the fact that the books are set in different locations to the TV programmes. In the novels, Vigàta is based on the author's home town of Porto Empedocle, but the TV shows naturally focus on the visual delights of Unesco World Heritage sites such as Scicli, Ragusa, Noto and Modica, all of which can be seen in the swooping helicopter shots in the opening credits. One option you have is to take a Montalbano coach tour, which can be very expensive indeed, but will show you the main sights.

Disappointingly, Salvo's house is privately owned, so you can only view the exterior, but the place we wanted to see was the Police Station, which is featured in every episode. It turned out that the town hall of Scicli was the location for the police station, but we didn't realise that, merely knowing that it was situated in Scicli (pronounced *sheek-ly*), in case you were wondering). Getting to Scicli was enough of a drama in itself.

The Sat Nav decided to have a double meltdown as we entered the town. We followed the instructions and embarked down a narrow road which we thought would take us to the town centre, only to find ourselves confronted by an enormous juggernaut, bearing down upon us from the opposite direction, hooting and flashing. Several pedestrians were pointing and gesticulating to show us that we were going the wrong way down a one-way street. As we were entirely in the wrong, we had to carefully reverse all the way back, something that isn't easy in a van with no back window. Luckily, the lorry driver didn't seem too angry.

We didn't know where the police station was likely to be,

so decided just to drive around until we found it. This poor policy took us over a railway line and down a rutted gravel track under a concrete bridge, which was only narrowly high enough for Polly to squeeze under. After the bridge, the road abruptly stopped at a brick wall and we had to do a very cautious ten-point turn in order to get out again. Shortly afterwards, we pulled up in front of a large pink building with several police patrol cars parked outside it and the word *Stazione* emblazoned on it. It was with a feeling of triumph that I took a photo of Polly parked on the forecourt of what was clearly Montalbano's headquarters. Sadly, when I smugly posted it on Facebook, I was immediately deluged with comments to the effect but it didn't look anything like the real thing. Well, as we now know, the real thing was, in fact, the town hall. Of course!

Ragusa is one of the principal Montalbano locations. It's quite beautiful. We found a precarious place to park and strolled through the steep cobbled alleys and down to the principal square in Ragusa Ibla, the ancient quarter, where huge, complicated lights were being set up ready for the Festival of San Giorgio. We toured the impressive basilica, up a long flight of steps, complete with its murals of said saint, known to us simply as George, slaying the ferocious dragon. Of course, we consumed an *arancini* (yes, I did dribble grease onto my shirt), gave some money to a crap busker (something I always do when I'm in a good mood), purchased the obligatory fridge magnet and peered into the A Rusticana restaurant, one of Salvo Montalbano's favourite eating places (allegedly). Finally, we discovered the Giardino Ibleo gardens and the quite beautiful San Vincenzo Ferreri church, which we were on a mission to find because a friend of Birgit's had recently got married there. One interesting aspect of this place was the fact that the music being played over its PA was quite modern, almost pop music, in fact, as compared to the sepulchral tones broadcast in most other churches.

Giorgio's festival is apparently quite something. It's a kind of harvest festival in reverse. Instead of thanking God for the harvest, the revellers are asking him to deliver a good one. In the morning, locals bring bread to the Basilica and later it's delivered to farmers and workers in the fields. Then, three evenings running, George's statue and a massive silver casket containing his relics are paraded through the streets. The procession takes place amongst a cacophonous backdrop of cannons, church bells, bands and finally an enormous fireworks display, as the statue is slowly carried up the Duomo staircase and returned to its plinth.

As for Saint George himself, whose spirit dominates the

town, well, Ragusa can no more lay claim to him than England can. He's actually claimed as a patron saint by Venice, Genoa, Catalonia and Portugal, among other places. In Ragusa, his Saint's Day is May 31, while St. George's Day in England is April 23. All agree that he was martyred by being executed because his virtue and holiness led him to refuse to make a sacrifice to a pagan god. As he was born in Turkey and died in Israel, it is conceivable that he might have visited Italy, but he certainly wouldn't have made it as far as England. Despite the fact that he died in AD 303, the myth of him slaying the dragon wasn't invented until the late thirteenth century. Why he merits having pretty much the entire town of Ragusa dedicated to him is unclear, but that's saints for you.

The route back along some quite challenging back roads took us through Modica, where we did that thing that tourists often do, which was to take a wrong itinerary that entirely avoided all the main sights. This particular one took us up a messy pathway, past derelict houses and to an eventual dead end, decorated tastefully with dog poo. So it was back to Camping Luminosa, where Toni's gas delivery enabled us to heat up a tin of Lidl ravioli, a sight that would have caused any Sicilian to faint in shock.

The following day was spent in a fruitless search for a

national park, which was flagged up in the guidebook as being of particular beauty and ecological interest. Our dependence on signposts was hindered by the complete lack of any. Eventually we arrived at Lido di Noto. Many towns in the area are inland, but have their own beach down the road at the coast, referred to as "Lido di Whatever". Lido di Noto was a nondescript beach with a concrete promenade and sadly, in contrast to the delightful nature reserve we had been led to expect, we found yet more awful litter and embarked on a very uninteresting walk through some heathland that had recently been completely destroyed by fire. Ugh, I can smell it as I type. Presumably, the promised nature reserve was somewhere in the area, but we never found it.

The next planned campsite was in a place called Avola, and turned out to be extremely difficult to access. Even the ACSI book warned about it being at the end of a narrow lane. So narrow was the lane that we initially missed it and had to drive on for three miles on a busy road before we were able to pull off and turn around. We found ourselves briefly in a roadside pull-in where some very dodgy deal was going down, and a couple of men strode threateningly over to us to make it clear that we had no business there. No worries, we were keen to exit as fast as possible.

The campsite owners were charming and an elderly

gentleman mounted his bike and led us down some tortuous slopes to a prime spot overlooking the sea - and without us having to pay extra. It all seemed fine until the time came for us to plug into the electricity. We promptly fused the entire row of vans, causing our German neighbours to accuse us of being the cause of the problem.

This was only one of many examples of people looking at our UK number plate and assuming we were troublemakers. In this case, the implication was that, with our darned different voltage and bloody three-pin plugs, we were messing up the entire system. I apologised profusely and then, with great difficulty, we manoeuvred the van up some steep, tight bends to another spot, where everything worked perfectly. We felt that we had now completed the Full House of breakdowns: first water, then gas and now electricity.

It was finally time to have a nice meal. As usual, the campsite was miles from civilization but it did have a restaurant, of which it was extremely proud, boasting of homemade local specialities. Perfect! So in we went and treated ourselves to a three-course meal which again - could this possibly be true? - appeared to come with free wine. This meal was the first in a series which went:

1. "Authentic Sicilian pizza, how wonderful!"

2. "Another pizza, how nice!"

3. "Hmmm ... pizza."

4. "Do we really have to have another pizza?"

5. "I'm never going to eat another pizza as long as I live."

This meal, however, was a major success, because when we came to pay for it, it turned out that their credit card machine was broken.

"Don't worry," we were assured. "You can pay at reception when you leave tomorrow."

Indeed, in the morning, I explained to the reception lady that we owed her forty euros for our meal, to which she responded that the machine was still broken and that therefore we didn't need to pay either for the overnight stay or the meal. My suggestion that I could drive to an ATM, come back and pay her in cash was waved away with a smile. For some reason, I think she liked us.

9

UP AND ETNA

There was a momentous start to the next day's diary: NOT DEAF in capital letters. Whoopee! We were headed for Catania, which was much anticipated because some very discerning and knowledgeable rock and rollers I know had recorded an album there and told us we absolutely must visit this amazing city. We were distinctly unamazed by the horrific traffic conditions, almost on a par with Palermo, but we made it to the campsite, which was on the seafront at the outer extremity of the city.

We were greeted by a super-efficient and professional lady, dressed in a smart black business suit. She was clearly starting a new job and wanting to make a good impression, so she insisted on leading us in person to what she told us was the best slot on the entire site. It was indeed spectacular, overlooking some jagged rocks and ideally positioned for a lovely sunset. Truth to tell, our lady was the only aspect of the site that wasn't run down and scruffy, but all the staff were very keen and welcoming.

We planned to stay there for a couple of days and were in the mood to chill. First we caught a bus into Catania (getting the tickets from a tobacco shop, of course) and checked out all the sights. Truth to tell, there weren't actually many of them, because of the city's terrible historical relationship with natural disasters. Originally founded in 729 BC and subsequently under Roman rule, the entire city was destroyed by an earthquake in 1169. There are minor traces of an amphitheatre still to be seen, but that's pretty much it. The city as it is today is the result of a catastophic eruption of Mount Etna in 1669, pretty much destroying any ancient buildings. The whole of Catania was buried under lava, and a mere thirty years later, another earthquake destroyed everything that remained. But the resilient inhabitants turned the disaster to their advantage. Unique in the world, and known as the "Grey City", present-day Catania is built entirely of grey and black lava and limestone, and is Baroque in character.

We felt very comfortable in Catania, as the vibe was so

different from the other ancient sites we had visited, but it's also a tense sort of place, still perpetually threatened by eruptions. The most recent one was on Boxing Day 2018, when a 4.8-magnitude earthquake, triggered by an eruption of Mount Etna, injured 28 people and damaged several buildings.

Everywhere we went in Catania, the name of Saint Agatha followed us. Her cathedral is one of the most prominent places of worship in the city (many are still in a poor state of repair and can't be visited). Agatha's feast day is on February 6, and is marked by a procession of relics that is attended by more than a million pilgrims and tourists. Even compared to the tribulations of St Rita, Agatha had quite a life, as can be deduced from the causes for which she is the Patron Saint: breast cancer, prevention of fire, rape victims and wet nurses. If you are of a nervous disposition, look away from the next paragraph.

Oddly, it's not known whether Agatha was born in Palermo or Catania, but the year was 231 AD. Allegedly a woman of great beauty, Agatha decided early on to become a Consecrated Virgin, remaining celibate and dedicating her life to Jesus. Unfortunately, being so attractive, her task was hindered by lustful men fancying her. One such was Quintianus, a high-ranking official, who tried to force her to marry him. When Agatha refused, he arranged for her to be arrested and brought before a judge, who just happened to be Quintianus himself. Faced with threats of torture, Agatha remained steadfast, upon which Quintianus had her sent to prison - in a brothel. When this didn't work either, Quintianus got stuck into the torture, having poor Agatha torn with iron hooks, stretched on a rack, burned with flaming torches, and whipped. When Agatha failed to be troubled by any of these methods, he finally ordered her breasts to be cut off. With the help of a vision of St Peter, Agatha's wounds were healed within four days.

You'd have thought that, at that stage, old Quintianus would have admitted defeat, but no, he had some more ideas in reserve. He had Agatha stripped naked and rolled over red-hot coals, mixed with razor-sharp stones, before returning her to prison, where she died in 251. Everywhere we went, we saw visual representations of Agatha, depicted with tongs, scissors and breasts on a plate, which was apparently how she liked to transport them after severance. We drew the line at the temptation to indulge in any *Minni di Sant Aita*, which are the bosom-shaped pastries, a local delicacy on sale in every bakery. The nipple is a glacé cherry.

It was in Catania that we saw the only sign of any dodgy dealings to be spotted on the entire trip. Outside the castle museum were small groups of intimidating youths, clearly carrying out drug transactions. We made up for that by finding a rather smart café opposite the Massimo Bellini opera house. The composer Salvatore Bellini, known as the "Swan of Catania" on account of the swooping nature of his melodies, wasn't originally from Catania, but has been adopted by the city. His operas are still regularly performed there. Not being opera fans, we instead indulged in some expensive Aperol Spritzes, complete with free platefuls of aperitif snacks.

When we got back to the campsite, we decided it was too late to cook anything, and so entered the site restaurant. This seemed to be run entirely by two young lads, who were also helping out on reception. When we ordered pasta with *ragù* (spaghetti Bolognese to you and me), we observed through the open kitchen door that they merely opened a packet of spaghetti and a jar of pasta sauce and mixed them up. So much for the claims on the menu that the food was to be home-cooked local specialities.

The next day was to be Etna day. Our well-dressed lady had set us up with a tour, which she assured us would collect us from the nearby main road at 9 a.m. We tried in vain to get her to tell us precisely where the bus would pick us up, and became very worried because we feared we were on the wrong side of the road. The rush-hour traffic was heading in the exact opposite direction to where we were supposed to be going. Fifteen minutes after we were due to be collected, we were about to give up, when suddenly a little bus appeared and screeched to a halt next to us. We joined a small group of tourists and were amazed to find ourselves being driven out of town to a seaside resort called Aci Castello, where we had half an hour to wander round. Then followed a full-scale city tour of Catania, conducted by our cheerful young driver Alessandro. He explained that this was the only way to get us from the campsite to the Etna tour, for which he was also the driver. Effectively, we were getting two tours for the price of one.

The bus filled up with more and more tourists from all over the world and we gradually ascended, first to the small town of Nicolosi for a coffee stop (Alessandro clearly had a deal with the café) and finally to Refugio Sapienza, which, at 2000 metres above sea level, is the highest point on the volcano that you can reach by coach. On the way, we saw a house buried up to its eaves in lava, that has been left to show tourists the extent of the devastation. The landscape is often described as "lunar", and certainly that is how desolate it feels.

As we drove up, it gradually became more cloudy and

cold. We had already been told by several people that it was unlikely to be worth spending the extra sixty euros each (yes, you read that correctly) to take the cable car to the actual summit and main crater, because the clouds would obscure any potential views. Two Russian girls in front of us on the bus were dressed in skimpy shorts and crop-tops, but Alessandro resisted their pleas to be allowed just to stay on the bus. Instead, they spent the allotted three hours shivering in a corner.

We successfully filled the time by visiting some of the smaller craters and delving down into one of them for a picnic, before taking a long walk through the rather depressing black lava. So dark was everything and so (I'm really sorry to have to say this again) litter-strewn that the Etna experience can be described as impressive and intimidating, rather than inspiring or uplifting. Considering it is one of the world's most famous tourist sites and natural phenomena, you'd think it would be at least worth employing the odd person with a pointed stick to go around picking up the rubbish, surely?

Back on our seafront slot, we created a boiled egg salad and a spectacular selection of very ripe cheese and declared ourselves happy. For entertainment, we watched a group of American scuba divers doing a course nearby. Being dramatically overweight, they all struggled to get in and out of their wetsuits but still managed to keep smoking cigarettes throughout the entire operation.

Now it was time to think about getting back to the Italian mainland. We had been assured by several different people that all you had to do was pitch up at the ferry port in Villa San Giovanni and buy a ticket there. This seemed potentially unreliable advice, so I used my phone to go online and purchase a ticket for a very reasonable 20 euros. On the way to Villa San Giovanni, we had the first in a series of diesel panics, as the low fuel light was on and all the petrol stations seemed to be closed. When we did eventually find one, it was "attended service" and we noticed a considerable premium on price compared to self-service. On the other hand, the proprietor gave me something I'd always wanted, one of those little cardboard clocks you put on the dashboard when doing street parking. I still don't know how to use it and whether you're supposed to indicate the time of arrival or the planned time of departure, but I've always been rather jealous of people possessing such an item, and proudly displayed it from then on.

Our final target in Sicily was Taormina. Here, we lucked out yet again with another premium-free seafront slot on a large, well-kept site. Once again, we were struck by the reluctance of other campers to want to interact with us. As with everywhere we had visited, it was almost entirely middle-aged couples from Germany, Holland and sometimes France. They would approach each other with alacrity and strike up acquaintanceships but, despite our smiles and nods, nobody seemed interested in us. It was hard to dispel the fear that this might possibly be Brexit-connected. Presumably they were assuming from our UK number plate that not only would we be unlikely to speak their language, we might also generally be anti-European in some way.

As we were near the entrance, we were able to observe another campsite phenomenon. Virtually all sites have very limited wi-fi and usually this extends a mere few metres around the reception area. Therefore, there is always a rather sinister-looking little group of people shuffling around, often in the dark, rather like the traditional smokers skulking outside any branch of Wetherspoons in the UK.

I made a point of going up to German and French campers and addressing them in their own languages, whereupon the expressions on their faces invariably turned to palpable relief. One German couple we met at the bus stop turned out to have lots I could relate to. They, too, had two grown-up daughters, a very inconspicuous van that they had saved up for and the husband came from Kiel, the German city

I spent time in as a student. It turned out we had plenty of time to chat at the bus stop, since the bus itself was 35 minutes late. This was predicted with uncanny accuracy by our new friends, who had done the same trip the day before and also had to wait 35 minutes then.

The bus took us into the very touristy town of Taormina, a place rather like the Amalfi coast in its precipitous hills and its embracing of the tourist euro. This was epitomised most clearly in the astronomical price charged to enter its amphitheatre. Am I a bad person for saying that one amphitheatre is actually very much like another, or that one plate of pasta or pizza is also very much like another, or, most pertinently, that one *duomo* a day really is quite sufficient? No, I'm simply a philistine.

Johann Wolfgang von Goethe, who spent time in Taormina during his tour of Sicily in 1787, was a lot more impressed by the amphitheatre than we were. Uncharacteristically for a poet and playwright, he was actually stumped for words: "Thank goodness everything we saw today has been sufficiently described already," was the best he could come up with. "We could not tear ourselves away until after sunset. To watch this landscape, so remarkable in every aspect, slowly sinking into darkness, was an incredibly beautiful sight." Well, to be fair, by sunset we were long gone.

As mentioned before, the whole of Taormina was as pristine as could be imagined, with not a speck of litter anywhere. As usual, all the thousands of tourists stuck rigidly to the main drag and ignored all the enticing side alleys. After skidding around and getting completely drenched in the amphitheatre, we set off on a walk to try to reach a castle, which was perched enticingly at the top of a cliff. Sure enough, we climbed hundreds of steps without encountering another soul, before arriving at a firmly locked castle door. Luckily, on the way, there was a delightful small church called Madonna della Rocca built into the rocks, where we sat for a few minutes' reflection.

We had actually hoped that these rest days would be taken up with lounging by a pool or on the beach, but as it was dull and cold, we decided just to sit around and read. In the distance, we could see a building a couple of miles up the coast, atop a hill. Needing exercise, we set off along the beach to see if we could reach it. We soon ran out of beach and had no alternative but to trudge for several kilometers along a busy dual carriageway, which had no pavement, before eventually reaching the Crystal Sea, which turned out to be a smart hotel.

"Do you serve coffee?" we asked the sole member of staff, who seemed taken aback by our sudden appearance.

The answer was in the affirmative and we were led on to a panoramic balcony. We were quite clearly the only guests in the entire building, but so pleasant was the experience that one coffee turned into a couple of Aperol Spritzes and the most outrageously expensive bill of the entire holiday: five euros for each small coffee and twelve euros for each cocktail. Clearly needing to economize, we devoted the evening to a bowl of soup and a game of Bananagrams.

The Sicilian experience had been half-and-half really, not as thrilling as we had expected, but with a good chunk of adventures and talking points. Mainly churches, to be fair.

---

(10)

COMMUNICATION BREAKDOWN

The crossing over the Strait Of Messina (probably not actually the most beautiful sea crossing in the world, as the guide book enthusiastically described it) was entirely without incident and only took about twenty minutes. The day's diary starts with the most extraordinary word, whose meaning I had all but entirely forgotten: SUN! How appropriate, therefore, that we had designated that day as a driving day. It turned out to be one on which very little was achieved.

The guidebook was very enthusiastic about an archaeological site called Sybaris. As it lay vaguely on our route towards the top of the "boot of Italy", we were determined to find it, but the palaver involved was quite ridiculous, involving numerous instances of backtracking, fruitless grilling of passers-by and a complete failure to find the place we were seeking.

I had a memory of the word *sybaritic*, but no idea what it meant, so looked it up. The definition was promising: "characterised by, or loving luxury or sensuous pleasure". Sybaris promised Roman ruins and baths, but all we found was an archaeological museum, which was shut. As we travelled around, dodging the many heavy lorries on the completely flat and featureless roads, the only sight to liven the day up was that of the numerous prostitutes, sitting on camp chairs amongst the garbage in the lay-bys, presumably to entice the lorry drivers from their cabs. We did notice one taxi driver who stopped and had a brief conversation with one of the ladies, who then entered his car and was driven off down a dark lane. It looked like the first minute of a typical episode of Silent Witness. All in all, it was pretty "sybaritic".

Meanwhile, we had run out of groceries and headed for a huge supermarket, where we were trapped for nearly an hour because the rain outside was so torrential that we could not get back to Polly. What? Oh, the sun hadn't lasted. We made up for the previous day's extravagance by having a coffee in the supermarket canteen, which was populated by large numbers of over made-up teenage girls, who were clearly in training for a career in the locality. Here, a much larger cappuccino than we had had the day before cost a mere one euro.

The campsite we found was a very cheap one in some woods by a lovely beach. We obeyed the orders of the receptionist, who pointed out an area where we weren't allowed to park, because a group was due to arrive the next day and had reserved it. Nonetheless, several other campers ignored his instructions, causing quite a stir when he came along and insisted that they move. They, of course, had to go through the whole unplugging process before they could co-operate. On the beach was a sole lifeguard in a highchair, quite unnecessary really, as we were the only other people to be seen. But we actually managed something that we had almost given up hope of, namely taking off our shoes and socks and paddling for a while.

It was clear that we had bitten off slightly more than we could chew in the way of the lengthy drives that were necessary to get us back up to Northern France in time for the return ferry we had booked. But sometimes it's when you are just driving along that you happen upon the best places. Today was such a day, as we stopped in Matera, one of the most amazingly beautiful places I have ever seen. Approaching the town, we had to take a sudden sharp left turn, following a sign for Tourist Information. This led us into a drab trading estate, where there was indeed a small tourist office. The lady in there was quite astonishingly unfriendly, unhelpful and unwelcoming. Not for the first time, we speculated on the motivations of people in the hospitality industry taking up a career for which they are so clearly temperamentally unsuited.

She did eventually reluctantly point out an extremely complicated route to a suitable car park and actually, in the end, we forgave her, because she had obviously drawn the short straw. Rather than spending the day with her colleagues in the picturesque town centre, she had clearly been delegated to work on her own in a crappy business park. It was plain to see that Matera was geared up for tourists, because there was a specially designated and rather swish camper van park. From there, it was a shortish walk into town. From the copious banners draped around the place, it was easy to spot that Matera, as well as being a World Heritage Site, was also 2019's European Capital Of Culture. That made me even more ashamed that I'd actually never heard of the place.

Matera is one of the oldest towns in the world, dating

from the Neolithic age. The ancient quarters, known as the *Sassi*, are hewn into a rocky area sitting over a massive limestone gorge. They consist of a mixture of caves and man-made dwellings. The creation of the cave dwellings can be dated back to the beginning of the eighteenth century. It was simply irresistible to enter the cave house that has been preserved in its original form to be experienced by the public. The cave is called the *Vico Solitario* and is in the *Sasso Caveoso*. A snip at two euros admission, it's like nothing else you've ever experienced.

You enter the vaulted room through a doorway, above which is the only window, which is so high that its purpose is clearly to provide air, rather than views. The whole construction is built into an excavated area and at the back of the dwelling, behind a partition wall, a stable for animals has been carved out, along with a manger against the wall. In the dwelling part, there's a large chest called the "wheat chest", divided into two compartments, one for wheat for human consumption and the other for animal fodder. In front of the bed is another store, with a trough for a mule or a horse, as well as space for chickens, a pig and other animals.

Since the cave was not equipped with toilet facilities, the inhabitants used a *cantera*, a painted terracotta chamber pot with a wooden lid, which was kept to the left of the bed. Furniture consisted mainly of a large bed for the parents. Covered with a wheat-filled mattress, this was very high, to keep it away from the humidity of the floor but also to utilise the space underneath it. This space was used to store items, and usually a mother hen and her chicks were kept there too. The smallest child slept at night in a crib at the foot of the bed. Another child slept with the parents and there was room for a further infant in the bottom drawer of a chest of drawers to the right of the bed.

The families who lived in these dwellings were usually large, with an average of six children, in spite of the fact that the infant mortality rate was around fifty percent. At mealtimes, the family all ate from a single large dish. Near the door is the opening of the cistern which contained the family's water reserves, and to the right you can see the channelling system which brought rain water to the cistern.

If you saw this sort of thing in a Heritage Museum, with huge families and farm animals all living together in squalor, you wouldn't bat an eyelid, but the incredible truth is that this way of life survived until 1952, when over fifteen thousand people began to be transferred to new houses being built in the modern city. Matera had become known world-wide as the "Shame Of Italy" because of the mediaeval conditions that people were living in, in the mid twentieth century. At that time, Matera had about 30,000 inhabitants, and the transfer of half the population occurred between 1953 and 1968. Many of the inhabitants didn't want to leave and certainly resented what they saw as an attack on their way of life.

The particular home we visited had been empty since 1956. The transfer was carried out by the Italian government, who swopped the original homes for brand new houses. Thus, they became the proprietors of the ancient dwellings. Seventy percent of the *sassi* are now owned by the State and managed by the local council. Now, they are undergoing restoration and renovation, and many of them are in the process of being turned into up-market restaurants and boutique hotels. Considering their humble beginnings, this seems ironic.

Feeling a little footsore, we sat down with a group of Japanese tourists to watch a video about Matera, which had been produced by the local tourist office. The climax was some frankly quite intimidating footage of an extraordinary festival that takes place annually on July 2.

During the festivities, a statue of the Virgin Mary is carried in procession on a float all afternoon along the crowded, narrow streets of Matera. On arrival at the square of the *duomo*, the carriers run three laps before placing the statue in the cathedral. Surrounding it are so-called "knights", which are mules and horses decorated with paper flowers and drapery. The huge statue, plus the chariot on which it is carried, which have taken months of craftsmanship to create, are then attacked and completely torn to pieces by crowds of local youths. To us, it looked like a scene of violent anarchy, but in Matera it is viewed as a normal activity. Then they set to work, building a new statue for the following year.

Left almost breathless by the incredible beauty of Matera, our good luck continued with a lengthy but picturesque drive through the olive groves of Puglia, ending up in a seaside resort called Specchiolla. This was a modern and well-appointed site with a huge swimming pool. As there were a number of pretty restaurants on the seafront, we made the probably flawed decision to go out for a pizza. A barely competent waitress delivered me a prawn pizza that contained no prawns. When I pointed this out, I reasonably expected that they would make me a new dish, but no, they merely defrosted a few prawns and scattered them on the top of the original pizza. They were not destined to be getting many stars from me on Trip Advisor.

The next day turned out to be the proverbial game of two halves. We had already been in a slight quandary about which way to go, having been strongly recommended to visit Lecce. As this was 100 kilometres or so in the wrong direction and the clock was ticking, we decided instead to tour the sights of Puglia. First stop, after a pretty horrible *autostrada* journey, was the almost unbearably idyllic hilltop town of Ostuni, where we bought scrumptious ice cream, numerous bottles of olive oil and even some clothes in advance of Birgit's birthday. Suddenly, from out of nowhere, we started hearing English voices for the first time in weeks. They were emanating from very well-dressed hipster types pushing expensive prams. One can only assume that they were spending time in their Puglian second homes.

Everywhere we drove was pretty, and the next place we arrived at was the legendary Alberobello, home of the world-famous *trullis*. There are over 1500 of these strange, conical buildings in Alberobello. We weren't quite sure where to park, but in the end settled for a street in the outskirts and set off in search of some *trullis*. We scoured the backstreets, occasionally finding the odd little beehive house but not the large groups of them that we had seen in tourist brochures. We had wasted quite a lot of time and I was getting increasingly concerned about the parking meter running out, when we eventually asked an American couple who showed us the way to the centre of Alberobello. This is indeed surely one of the wonders of the world. Draped up the hill are scores of *trullis*, arranged along a series of cobbled streets, which were in the process of renovation.

Made over thousands of years, using the dry-stone technique (i.e. without mortar), the *trullis* are whitewashed with lime and were originally constructed as shelters or dwellings for agricultural workers. The walls are thick, with double skinned roofs, fireplaces and alcoves. What makes them so fascinating is the way they cluster in groups, like stone flocks of sheep. When they ran out of inside space, they simply added another *trulli* next door and knocked through. *Trullis* are highly protected and the banning of inappropriate modern development in the centre of Alberobello lends a magical air to the whole place. Sure, it is ultra-twee, a bit like places such as Bourton-on-the-Water or Clovelly, which are preserved in aspic. Nonetheless, we absolutely loved the place, because it's not like anywhere else in the world.

We took pity on a poor lady whose café was cut off and obscured by the massive roadworks and she treated us to some local food and drink. Adding to the atmosphere were some pitch-black clouds looming large over the town, and before too long, they had decided to dump their contents onto us. Huddling under an umbrella, we made it back to the van, eager for its shelter. We jumped in, slammed the doors and Birgit inserted the ignition key.

You know that sound made by an engine as it turns over but does not start? I'm not much good at phonetics but the sound is a bit like this:

"Oof, oof, oof ..."

"Hmm, strange ..."

"Oof, oof, oof oof, oof ..."

"What the hell?"

"Oof oof oof oof oof oof ..."

"Shit!"

One thing that had been nagging at my paranoid mind for weeks had been, "Okay, actually everything else has broken down, so what if Polly's engine goes?" I'd managed to suppress it so far, but the refusal of the engine to start brought all my fears rushing to the surface. Oh God, what on earth could we do? It was pouring with rain, it was a Saturday, for goodness sake, it was late afternoon. We would somehow have to contact our insurance company. Oh Christ, we would have to be transported back home on the back of a lorry. We probably wouldn't be covered. The entire rest of the holiday would be ruined. We would have to find and pay for a hotel for days before we could be rescued. We would be bankrupted. Shit, oh God, Christ, help. Maybe visiting so many churches had made it so natural to invoke the Lord.

All I knew about getting cars to start when they don't want to was the concept of "bump starting", where you push a vehicle downhill, whack it into gear and release the clutch, but I knew also that that system was only applicable when the battery was dead. In this case, we knew for certain that the battery was brand new, and if it had been dead, the engine wouldn't be making any noises at all. And besides, we were positioned between two other parked cars, facing uphill on a one-way street. That was the limit of any potential I had for solving the problem.

When we had parked up, I had felt slightly hesitant because we were directly opposite what looked like a dodgy drinking den, a scruffy bar with a few blokes hanging around outside it, smoking and drinking. Now, amidst the panic, these were the only people I felt I could turn to. I first jogged up the road to a petrol station that we had passed, but, predictably, it was unmanned and self-service only. Back at the bar, only one drinker remained, a large, intimidating looking gentleman who was studying us closely. He seemed interested in our efforts to get Polly started. Hesitantly, I crossed the road and approached him.

"Inglese?"

He shook his head. Er ... What else could I say? I pointed to the car, shrugged my shoulders and said,

"Meccanico?"

To my total amazement, he nodded and said "sì". Surely I hadn't found a *meccanico* at the first attempt? I was right, I hadn't. He reached into his pocket, pulled out his mobile phone and dialled a number. After about a minute's conversation, he replaced the phone, looked at me and nodded.

"Cinque minuti."

As the potential for further conversation was minimal, I gave him a thumbs up, which I am aware is not necessarily an international signal of pleasure, and returned over the road to Birgit.

"I'm not entirely sure, but as far as I understand it, a mechanic is going to arrive in five minutes."

Exactly five minutes later, a car screeched to a halt next to us and a large, swarthy gentleman got out. He tapped the bonnet of Polly and made a signal for us to open it. He then disappeared into the engine and started fiddling around rather roughly with various cables and other bits and pieces. I could hardly bear to look, but I did, in increasing horror, because diesel was squirting around and he had a lit cigarette dangling from his lower lip. Eventually, he found something that looked a bit like a human heart, in that it was rubbery, malleable and had things like arteries going in and out of it.

He squeezed this hard and a stream of diesel came squirting out.

"Sì," he pronounced, reached into his pocket and pulled out his phone. Using the now increasingly life-saving Google Translate, he held the phone up to me so I could read the words "Fuel Pump".

"Sì," I agreed, attempting to give the impression that I had the slightest idea what a fuel pump was or did. Tap tap tap, he went again on this phone. "Follow me," said the words, as he leapt back into his car and started moving away up the road. He'd improvised a temporary bodge on the offending component that allowed the engine to start. There followed a hair-raising itinerary down some narrow side streets and an eventual arrival in a small industrial estate, containing six or seven different types of mechanics' workshops. He signalled to us just to sit in the van and wait. At this stage, I really thought it was necessary to find out his name, and established that he was called Gianni.

Other than that, he didn't seem remotely interested in any kind of communication or conversation, so we had no indication of how long it might take or what it might involve, and - the potential killer - how much it was going to cost. There was nothing for it but to sit tight. We could see that he was working simultaneously on three different cars. One was having its tyres changed, one was having something done to its headlights and one was having a dent repaired.

After about forty minutes, another vehicle appeared and delivered a box with something in it. Gianni removed the item and disappeared back under our bonnet with various tools. Shortly afterwards, he popped his head out and announced, "Finito."

At this stage, he showed us the old heart-like object that he had removed, and pointed at the brand new one that his friend had delivered and that he had just installed. Inviting us to switch on the engine, he smiled for the first time, as it instantly burnt burst into life, sounding as healthy as if nothing had happened. It certainly would have been undignified for me to cuddle Gianni, but we blessed him with some radiant smiles and body language indicating abject gratefulness.

Now for the big one: What was it going to cost? Our relationship with him had improved dramatically when Birgit engaged him in a sign language exchange on the subject of some famous Italian footballers whose posters adorned the workshop wall. I think we shot up in his estimation at that moment. With a questioning look on my face, I rubbed finger and thumb together in order to try and elicit what we would have to pay. He did that typical mechanic thing of scratching his head, stroking his chin and typing some figures into a calculator. Eventually, he held up the calculator display to reveal the sum of 75 euros. Considering that I had been fearing several hundred, this was something that we had to grab instantly, but I only had 70 euros in cash.

"Prego, non c'è problema," announced Gianni and, amidst much shaking of hands and slapping of backs, we were able to get back on the road. In the kindness and generosity stakes, a competition between Graham in East Sussex and Gianni in Alberobello would have been a close run thing.

Back at the campsite, we were in the mood for celebration. There was a pool bar that was being used by absolutely no one, and the two girls running it clearly had the best job in the world. They merely sat around all day, eating and chatting and not doing any serving because there were no customers. I inquired whether they knew how to make an Aperol Spritz and, after consulting a cocktail book, that said they did. The sun had resumed, so we plunged into the pool, where we were the sole swimmers, before downing a couple of Spritzes and opening a packet of Miracoli. Miracoli is a German item, consisting of some spaghetti and a packet of tomato sauce with so-called secret spices. It's absolutely delicious, probably terribly bad for you and certainly not in the least bit Italian, but we didn't care.

Most normal holidays' daily diary entries would read, "Got up, ate, lounged by pool, ate again, swam, read, lounged by pool again, ate, drank, went to bed". And that's exactly what the next day entailed. No sightseeing, no shopping and, above all, no disasters. Result! That's all there was to say about that day, apart from two issues at the restaurant we chose for supper. Their version of "fish and chips" was utterly inedible and secondly, for some reason, my debit card refused to work when we tried to pay.

It was time to move on. On the route we chose, we noticed that there were some famous caves that could be visited. The *Grotte di Castellana* were presented as a full-on commercial tourist attraction, but the sun had come out and was smiling on us, so we didn't care. Something I rapidly did start to care about was the non-functioning of my debit card. After the credit card fiasco a few weeks earlier, I'd just had time to transfer all my money into my current account, in order to use my debit card, but as I tried to pay the very expensive admission fee to the *grotte*, the card was refused.

We were in the classic situation where the lady at the counter gave me a severe stare and the people behind us nudged each other, clearly thinking, "This guy's dodgy". It was essential to get the card going again, so we sat in the sweltering car park as I tried to contact my UK building society's helpline. Anyone who has ever attempted such a thing will be familiar with the labyrinthine depths of saccharin music and button pressing that entailed. When I eventually got through to a human being, what I heard was quite extraordinary.

"Yes, sir, every now and then we send out a new debit card to our customers. It's a security measure."

"Did you have any reason to think that there was a security problem with my card?"

"No, sir, it's just routine."

"I see. Please would you be so kind as to reverse this because I'm now stuck in Italy with a non-functioning debit card."

"I'm sorry, sir, that's not possible."

"Why not?"

"Because the card has been deactivated and can't be reactivated."

"But before I left, I filled in an online form telling you I was going to be going abroad. I told you the exact dates I would enter and leave each country."

"Ah, well, that's a different department."

It was a classic case of "computer says no", and I was getting riled as hell.

"Don't worry, sir, we've sent you a replacement card."

"Where did you send it to?"

"To your home address. It will be there waiting for you when you get back."

He didn't seem to think that was any kind of problem.

Warning him that I was going to be sending a severe letter of complaint to the company, I did the modern-day equivalent of slamming down the phone in fury, which means I stabbed my finger a little bit more harshly than usual onto the screen. I did, in fact, have another bank account but there was no money in it, so the next half an hour had to be spent juggling cash from deposit account to current account online. It was a miracle that we had any signal to enable me to do this, because much of the time on this trip there hadn't been one available.

I know this is becoming a familiar theme, but one set of impressive *grotte* is very much like another. You are led down dank, subterranean corridors which are lit up to make them more atmospheric. You skid on the algae, graze your head on rocky protrusions and try to remember the difference between a stalactite and a stalagmite, while coming to terms with the fact that they grow by one millimetre every thousand years (or something like that). We had already seen the most spectacular *grottes* imaginable the year before, in the form of the *Grottes de Bétteram* in France. There, the dark and dank caverns were enlivened by underground trains and boats. The *Grotte de Castellana* are only really of interest to someone who's never seen any *grotte* before. Bloody expensive too.

The afternoon brought another diesel incident. We had sworn blind that we would never again get ourselves into a situation where we needed fuel where there were no petrol stations. Bugger me, that's exactly what we did. Having passed numerous garages and, in each case, decided that there was going to be another one round the corner, we ended up in a state of total panic, as the road stretched on for ever and ever with no sign of any buildings at all. We were heading for the oddly named town of Manfredonia, but had to strike out in a different direction in order to find somewhere to fill up. The sense of relief was palpable when we eventually found salvation in the form of an extraordinary filling station attendant, who wanted to practise his English on us:

"Hello John. You are John. I am Paolo. You are English. I am Italian. You are very nice, John. You are very English."

I smiled encouragingly, in order to support his false impression that all English people are nice.

MALFUNCTION

The next day, I was plagued by earworms, you know, songs that won't leave you in peace. On this occasion it was a triple-header of "5-4-3-2-1", "The Mighty Quinn" and "Semi-Detached Suburban Mr James", all brought on by visiting Manfredonia. Some people's minds work in strange ways.

Today had been designated as a long driving day. In one of the few pieces of controversy between me and Birgit on the entire trip, I had requested to return to the scene of one of the most wonderful days of my life. This had taken place during our first Polly Pocket trip, four years previously. We'd spent a couple of nights on an idyllic campsite near Opi, in the Abruzzo mountains, and now I begged to be allowed to return. It was a long way off our route and entailed a lot of extra tortuous driving for Birgit, but eventually she agreed.

Back then, we'd decided to walk from the campsite to Opi, because the guide book said it was a nice town. But there was a problem. The campsite dog, called Malfu, decided to come with us. Neither of us likes dogs, but no amount of scolding, shooing or shouting would put him off. He was going to accompany us no matter what. This was frightening at first, because the start of the hike was on a road and he kept running across in front of cars. But as we entered the national park, we thought maybe it wasn't so bad he was with us after all, because of the signs everywhere warning of bears.

The paths we were trying to follow were badly marked with every chance of getting lost, but Malfu seemed to know where we wanted to go. At times, he would disappear for a few minutes and we'd think we were rid of him (now, of course, worrying that he would not find his way home), but he'd always reappear, on one occasion bringing two stags whom he'd startled into running right in front of us. After a couple of hours, he brought us to our destination, Opi, the most perfect hilltop town imaginable. The word "unspoilt" doesn't do this place justice. It literally seemed unchanged since mediaeval times, with its near vertical cobbled alleyways, its complete lack of anything modern or commercial and its almost spooky emptiness. We found somewhere for a coffee and Malfu dutifully waited outside, before leading us back to the campsite by a completely different route and delivering us back to Polly Pocket. When I asked the campsite owner if this was a common occurrence, he said, "He'll only do it if he decides he likes you".

It was too much to hope that Malfu would still be around, but the campsite, centred round a functioning water mill at the bottom of a mountain-fringed valley, was thankfully completely unchanged. As we set up, I heard Birgit's voice:

"Oh, hello darling!"

For a second, I thought I'd got lucky, but there Malfu was, snuffling round our toes as if we'd never been away. We are absolutely not "dog people" but something about this seemed deeply spiritual. Malfu definitely remembered us, of that there could be no doubt. Somehow, he had just chosen us. He showed no interest in any of the scores of other campers, and settled down outside the van to wait for us. Of course, another hike was essential, and there was an extraordinarily joyful sense of *déjà vu* as we set off along the road. The same bunch of dogs barked as we went by, the same goats bleated at us over the fence, even the same motorcyclist overtook us (okay, I made that one up).

We decided to take a different route through the National Park this time, and again, Malfu accompanied and guided us faithfully, even joining in our picnic. As I lay in the shade of a tree and dozed, he made sure I was alive by licking my face. I bloody hate dogs licking me - but not Malfu.

He got us worried by disappearing when he spotted a group of schoolchildren, who probably offered him more entertainment. We didn't see him again until back at the site, and were worried he might have got lost. Of course not; after half an hour, he bounded up, reassured us that all was well by rubbing himself against our legs and returned to his spot near the entrance, to continue to watch the world go by. We celebrated by entering the campsite restaurant, where we noticed with pleasure that the same eccentric owner-and-waitress combo as four years ago was still in place. We consumed a gorgeous meal (truffles, yum) and agreed that the detour had been more than worth it.

The next day was Sunday and the roads were nice and quiet for a beautiful drive through the Abruzzo mountains, only interrupted by the occasional suicidal motorcyclist screaming past or towards us. Just outside Narni, near the half-completed Roman viaduct, we found our quaint wooded campsite, which boasted a freezing cold but very bracing outdoor pool. Next to us was an English couple who were on a motorbike tour, but they showed absolutely no interest in communicating with us. Yet another "local speciality" restaurant failed to deliver, as it was closed for a children's party.

Narni was another hilltop settlement, this one with its own public elevator to whisk you up from the car park into the town centre. Oddly enough, several of the souvenir shops seem to be trading on the name's similarity to Narnia although, as far as I can tell, there is no connection between the two. Founded by the Romans in 209 BC, Narni was augmented during the twelfth century by the construction of seven churches and a cathedral. The town grew rapidly and the fourteenth century saw the creation of three Norman convents by the Dominicans, Franciscans and the Augustinians, and the Pope constructed a huge fortress. There was clearly enough institutionalized religion here to rival the Vatican City, but we just gave thanks to God for leading us to a lovely café that served an Italian version of a *mille-feuilles*.

Now we were entering Tuscany, instantly recognisable from the pointy cypress trees dotted around the landscape. Our destination was Siena and a campsite that we had chosen because it was on a bus route. This was proven by the fact that we were stuck behind a very slow bus all the way from Siena to the village where the campsite was situated. It was a very busy road with steep hills and vicious bends, so I intervened when, at the reception, a German family enquired whether they could cycle into Siena.

"I wouldn't recommend it, as the road is steep and dangerous," I commented.

The imperious lady of the family turned and fixed me with a stare of utter contempt.

"But our bicycles are with electricity," she announced, witheringly, before turning on her heel and marching out.

As we cooked our pasta supper, Birgit told me that she was sure she could hear bagpipes playing. This seemed highly unlikely, but sure enough, out in the middle of an adjacent field, there was a gentleman wailing away on the unspeakable instrument. Later on, it emerged that he was a Frenchman from Brittany and, with a minimal amount of encouragement, he staged an impromptu bagpipe concert in the car park, surrounded by a small but enthusiastic audience. Several of them struck up a friendship which developed into quite a rowdy party immediately adjacent to us. We would have quite fancied a rowdy party actually, but as usual were not invited.

The morning heralded a day out in Siena, but prior to that, there was a duty to carry out that is probably the one remaining aspect of camper van life that I have not got round to describing, mainly because it's not very pleasant. If you are, like us, not as young as you used to be, it's vital to have some kind of toilet facility in your van, unless you want to tiptoe around a campsite in your pyjamas in the middle of the night. We have a small but reasonably efficient Elsan chemical loo. It's called chemical, I guess, because you have to use two different coloured liquids with it, one pink one, which serves as a flush, and one bright blue one, which alleviates the smell.

Every campsite will have a chemical toilet disposal unit, basically a hole in the ground, but it's very important not to try and dispose of your waste anywhere else. Pouring it into a bush would be ecologically unsound, considering all the chemicals, and disposing of it down a regular loo is strictly forbidden. You also have to be careful while replenishing it with water. You obviously can't use the hosepipe provided for drinking water, as you might contaminate it. I always make a point of being meticulous about only using official disposal points, but on many campsites they can be hard to find, often tucked away on the extremities. Anyway, on this site near Siena, I received the answer to a question that I had never actually asked, namely, do people use their Elsans for anything other than wee-ing? We certainly don't, but here I discovered that plenty of people obviously do. This was revealed by the fact that the disposal tank was blocked and overflowing contents that I certainly wouldn't want to describe to any sensitive reader. Suffice to say that it got the day off to a less than pleasant start.

The journey into Siena was to take place on a normal service bus, which pulled up into the campsite yard in a cloud of dust. Interestingly, the German family joined us too, and their "bikes with electricity" remained firmly strapped to the back of their enormous camper van. Maybe they'd heeded my words of wisdom after all. For some reason, a large number of campers wanted to go into town on that day, but a particularly small bus had been scheduled. Before it even started its route into the city, it was absolutely crammed with people squashed up against each other. As we progressed along the bus route, normal commuters joined us. The driver simply pressed the button to open the doors and let everybody push their way in. It was like the London underground in the rush hour, but worse. Next to us was a Dutch couple whose van was parked near ours. They had something like a shopping trolley but instead of containing shopping, it contained - you've guessed it - their dog. I was hard pressed to decide whether it was more cruel to leave it in the van to be asphyxiated, or to drag the unfortunate creature round the Tuscan tourist trail.

The day out in Siena was a delight, but left us quite footsore. The heart of the city is the Piazza Del Campo. Each year, in July and August, it plays host to the Paleo, a historical procession preceded by a crazy and violent horse race. The amazing sense of architectural unity of the buildings surrounding the piazza is down to a law made in 1297, forbidding the building of balconies and insisting on the construction of mullioned windows. Worldwide, this is one of the first examples of city-centre architectural regulations being enacted.

The piazza is divided into nine segments and, as the whole thing is on a slant, the area suggests the shape of a seashell. It's dominated by the *Palazzo Pubblico* and the *Museo Civico*, which is one of the most important Gothic buildings in the world. Much of it is open to the public as a museum, and works of art we saw included incredible frescoes attributed to Martini in the breathtaking *Sala del Mappamondo*.

Adjacent to the Palazzo is the 520-step bell tower, which we puffed up and were rewarded with incredible views over the ochre-coloured city. Called the *Torre del Mangia*, it was built between 1325 and 1349 and was named after its first watchman, by all accounts quite a nasty piece of work. Fierce attendants made you leave everything in a locker at the bottom, for fear of people chucking stuff off the top. This included bottles of water, so there were some quite parched tourists when they returned to ground level.

As we were restricted to one day, we could only scratch the surface of the incredible buildings of Siena, including the *Porta Romana*, the Basilica of Santa Maria and the entrancing Sanctuary of Santa Catarina. The entire city is in such a perfect state of preservation that it easily rivals Florence as a tourist destination. Once the size of Paris, Siena now has a population of less than sixty thousand. This dates back to the devastating plague of the Black Death, which wiped out almost the entire population in the mid-fourteenth century.

Legend has it that Roman Siena was originally established by Senius, the son of Remus and nephew of Romulus. Therefore, the symbol of Siena is a she-wolf breastfeeding Romulus and Remus. Statues and other depictions of this odd procedure can be spotted all over the city.

Having somewhat overdosed on *duomos* in the last few weeks, we decided not to enter and instead, queued for the *Santa Maria Della Scala* gallery, which was incredibly rewarding. Having served as Siena's main hospital for nine hundred years, today its huge rooms have been converted into a hugely impressive art gallery, whose highlight is the gigantic

Sala del Pellegrunaio, which shows startlingly realistic scenes from the history of the hospital and its dedication to caring for sick people and orphans. We were also dumbfounded to discover in there an extraordinary painting of the Tower of Babel by Albrecht Dürer. It was fascinating to compare this slightly intimidating portrayal of linguistic chaos with another similar, and more famous, version by Pieter Breugel, which we had seen years before in the *Kunsthistorisches Museum* in Vienna.

One of the most memorable paintings was the *Cattivo Governo*, portraying a devil-like creature symbolising tyranny. The accompanying explanation sets out the principles of "Bad Government", which made such an impression on me that I noted it down: *"Concerned with protecting its own interests rather than the common good, it is aided by the worst vices in order to pursue its selfish plan. It has neutralized justice, disenfranchising its rules and its very dignity. Bad Government produces decisive negative effects in both the city and the countryside, and a fundamental fear in citizens, who see danger to their property, their activities and their very lives compared to the safety and guarantees of Good Government"*. Considering the state of the UK to which we were shortly to return, it seemed remarkably pertinent.

In the basement of the Santa Maria Della Scala, we found the Archaeological Museum. It was so enormous that we must have walked miles among the endless ruins on display. At one stage, Birgit got so tired that she sat down and let me continue on my own, which led to a number of bizarre and hilarious encounters with a Japanese couple who, like me, had got completely lost. We kept turning round corners and bumping into each other. As we couldn't communicate in any other way, we simply giggled.

Siena is an ideal place for aimlessly wandering along narrow, sloping streets, and we eventually found what we thought would be the ideal restaurant for the long awaited gourmet meal. We ended up in a rather smart *Osteria*, which had a delightful ambience but, well, pasta is pasta, isn't it? I know a few people who will never talk to me again after reading this.

In the archaeological museum, I came up against a moral dilemma. When I was a schoolboy, we once had an assembly about honesty. I always remember the headmaster telling us that if we found a penny on the floor and failed to hand it in to the police, it was, strictly speaking, theft. Since then, I have spent a lifetime being probably over-obsessively honest. In the depths of the museum, I sat down on a bench for a rest and noticed that there was an abandoned pair of Ray-Bans next to me. I was actually in dire need of some sunglasses, having broken my existing ones, but now there was a moral choice to be made. There were three alternatives: I could leave the Ray-Bans there in the hope that the owner would come back to retrieve them if he or she could possibly find a way through the impenetrable labyrinth. Alternatively, I could take them to the front desk and hand them in, in case the owner returned and asked if they had been found. Finally, I could simply pocket them. I chose the last of these options, on the basis that my headmaster was long dead, and that anyone who could afford to buy one pair of Ray-Bans could probably afford to buy another. It was all immaterial really because, when I got home, my daughter laughed and informed me that they were female sunglasses and I couldn't possibly wear them. I, of course, had had no idea that sunglasses came in male and female versions. Two days after returning home, I lost them anyway.

The bus designated for the return journey was happily a lot larger than the morning one, and we were able to compare notes with the Dutch couple. When they were unable to name any churches or museums they had visited, I asked them why.

"It wasn't possible because he has a bad leg," said the wife.

"Oh, I'm so sorry," I sympathized, turning to the husband. "I didn't realise you had an injury."

"It's not me," he replied, "it's the dog."

Some people really are slaves to their pets.

---(12)---

GIMME SOME LOVIN'

The following day was spent on beautiful small roads traversing the Tuscan landscape. Our destination was Lucca. Situated not far from Pisa, it's been a successful city since Roman days, with industries such as olive oil and silk. It's a well-to-do sort of place, and basks in its reputation as the birthplace of the composer Puccini in 1858.

Lucca is most notable for its spectacular and intact city walls, which completely enclose it. The thing that tourists do is hire bicycles and do a circuit, which only takes about half an hour. The problem is that the tourists come from all over the world and have completely different understandings of cycling etiquette. Basically, it's mayhem, with people not knowing what side of the path to be, what speed to maintain and which direction to ride in. I was aware that a friend of ours, just weeks before, had ended up in a Lucca hospital, being treated for broken limbs after a head-on collision. We both completed our circuit with extreme caution.

In the afternoon, we ended up in a gorgeous spa town called Montecatini Terme, where the campsite had quite a spectacular swimming pool. We hung out there for a good few hours and tried out some sangria that the campsite owner had made. In a sign that the off-season was coming to an end, the campsite and pool were actually quite busy, a phenomenon we had not previously encountered.

Now we were embarking on our last day in Italy, and as we had a lot of ground to cover, it was a long hard drive on a boring *autostrada* for Birgit to tackle. We were rewarded by a beautiful, brand-new campsite at Terlargo, near Trento, in the Dolomites. Surrounded by snow-capped mountains, we enjoyed our last swim in the sunshine, while dealing with yet another technical issue: Birgit's vital Kindle gave up the ghost, developing a pitch-black blob instead of a screen. Fortuitously, a previous German guest had left behind, at reception, a paperback *"Krimi"*, which lasted her until she got home.

I had a rather awkward social encounter here. We had scarcely come across another UK citizen on the entire trip, but as we pulled in to the campsite, we were approached by an elderly Scottish gentleman. He'd noticed the S on our number plate, dating back to the fact that Polly had been first registered in Scotland. To be frank, I was already beginning to feel the first stirrings of Brexit anxiety, knowing that we were going to be home in about a week. This meeting did nothing to help, because within two minutes, this man had already complained bitterly about three things:

1. The fact that the campsite receptionist didn't speak very good English. (I asked him how his Italian was and he huffed.)

2. The fact (in his mind) that petrol in Italy was more expensive than in the UK. (In fact, I soon realised that he was comparing euro and pound prices without doing any conversion.)

3. The fact that there HADN'T been any passport checks at the borders of the various mainland European countries they had visited. (I mentioned the concept of Shengen but he didn't seem to relate to it.)

So it was a tetchy moment at the pool when he and his wife plonked themselves down on sun loungers next to us, where he immediately began talking to her in a very denigrating and disparaging manner. We pointedly picked up our towels and moved to the opposite side of the pool. By dinner time, he had got the message and when they entered the restaurant, the two of them went and sat as far as possible away from us.

The dinner? Well, we had reached stage 5 on the pizza tolerance scale and, while it was perfectly adequate, felt no requirement to eat any pizza for the next few months. The grappa, to be fair, was another matter. We enjoyed it so much that we bought a large bottle the next day to take home with us.

Now it was time to tackle the Alps and, as we were in a hurry this time, it had to be motorways rather than winding mountain passes. We fell into a trap that is hard to avoid. The A22 Brenner pass motorway spends only a few kilometers inside Austria but for Austria you have to buy a *vignette*, which permits you to drive there. We were not best pleased to discover two extra downsides to this: First, that on top of the *vignette*, you also had to pay a substantial motorway toll, and secondly, that roadworks meant several hours of immobility in traffic jams. We had no alternative but to seek a different route, which was also plagued by holes in the road and temporary traffic lights, but at least we found a nice picnic spot by the Achensee lake.

We were headed for the Tegernsee in South Germany, and now I will explain why. In my teens, I was a big follower of the Spencer Davis Group, an extraordinary combination of unlikely chart toppers. In the band were singer, guitarist and keyboard player Steve Winwood, who was only fifteen when they started out, and sixteen when they began having hits. Other members included Steve's brother Muff and the eponymous Spencer Davis himself who, despite having the band named in his honour, was arguably the least talented member. He impressed me, however, because he was a German teacher, and somehow I later ended up doing the same.

On the drums was a slightly older but extraordinarily talented jazz musician called Pete York, whom I admired greatly for his work on unforgettable hits such as "Somebody Help Me", "Gimme Some Lovin'", "I'm A Man" and many more.

Who would have thought that one day our paths would cross? In the 1990s, I wrote a book called *Volume*, which somehow got into the hands of a keyboard player called Eddie Hardin. When Steve Winwood quit the Spencer Davis group in 1967, it was Eddie who replaced him on Hammond organ, beating several luminaries, including Terry Reid and Elton John, to the post. When that version of the Spencer Davis group split in 1968, Eddie formed a dynamic duo with drummer Pete York. They called themselves Hardin and

York and were dubbed with the title "The World's Smallest Big Band". For a while they were indeed big, especially in continental Europe and particularly in Germany, where I saw them a few times and became a loyal fan. So it was extraordinarily exciting when Eddie contacted me and asked if I would be willing to help him write his autobiography. During the course of this process, I had the pleasure and honour of meeting Pete York, and we stayed in touch.

One thing you need to know about me and Birgit is that, if you invite us to come and visit, we surely will do so. So think carefully before issuing such an invitation. Pete, over the years, had made the mistake of saying, "You really must visit us some time", and now the time had come.

Pete lives with his charming German wife Mecky in a beautiful house near the banks of the Tegernsee, a famously affluent area. Not wanting to impose too much on their hospitality, we had identified a non-ACSI camp site which turned out to be just a few minutes' walk from the Yorks' home. The site itself was not one of the better ones we had visited, catering mainly for long-term campers, who looked askance at us. We immediately got told off for parking in a spot where our electricity cable had to cross a path before being plugged in.

"We don't do that sort of thing here," pronounced our

neighbour, frowning. This didn't seem very welcoming, so we moved to a quiet corner of a deserted field nearby. Within an hour, a fleet of cars and vans rolled up and disgorged around twenty teenagers, who seemed to be visiting the Tegernsee for some kind of sports camp. Ignoring the vast expanses of space elsewhere, they set themselves up, almost like a wagon train encircling us, and proceeded to build an encampment of gazebos and to construct barbecues and unpack crate after crate of alcohol. We are not going to have a very peaceful night, we thought, and that turned that to be true, but not for the reason we expected. During the night, gale force winds suddenly blew up and the whole campsite was engulfed by horizontal, torrential rain. It was actually quite frightening, even for us in our van, so for those youngsters in their tents it must have been terrifying. They actually hadn't been partying at all, but when the storm struck, their gazebos got blown away and they had to retreat into their vehicles for safety. We actually felt really sorry for them.

The next day, we had been invited to visit the Yorks for a barbecue lunch. We wandered around the opulent streets, looking at expensive clinics where people come for their *Kur* or spa treatments, before being welcomed by Pete and Mecky. Mecky turned out to be a fascinating character, having being a socialite in the sixties. She ran a succession of successful high-class restaurants, first near London, where her clients would include rock stars like Deep Purple, and then near Munich, where Pete first met her and customers included David Niven, Peter Sellers, Sammy Davis Jr, Gina Lollobrigida and Franz Beckenbauer. Another rather thrilling tale was that Mecky turned down the rôle in Michelangelo Antonioni's 1966 film "Blow Up" that was eventually given to Jane Birkin. Mecky refused the job because she was unwilling to undress for the cameras.

Both Pete and Mecky are incredible raconteurs, and Birgit and I were transfixed with the riveting tales of rock star life, none of which I am prepared to divulge here. One of the best stories, however, was closer to home. Their house is a typically German *Doppelhaus*, (semi-detached to us) and they explained how they had come to acquire it. In the other half of the house still lives an old lady in her nineties. One day a few years ago, the lady invited the couple who then lived in the other half of the house out for a drive, and parked up by the Tegernsee. When the time came to drive home, she mistakenly put the car into reverse instead of first gear, and the car plunged backwards into the lake. The two neighbours in the back seat were drowned, while she herself, being in the front seat, which wasn't submerged, survived. That is how Pete and Mecky's house became available for purchase.

After the barbecue, Pete gave me one of the most thrilling experiences of my life, as he invited me into his cellar studio, where he does a three-hour drum workout every day, even though he's in his mid-seventies. In the studio there are two drum kits and a recording and rehearsal setup, all decorated by unique photographs and posters from a long and successful career. In recent years, Pete has been the drummer for a famous German comedian and jazz pianist called Helge Schneider.

If you've never thought of Germany as a holiday destination, think again. Especially in Bavaria, there is a plethora of utterly gorgeous unspoilt mediaeval towns which fill me with emotion, because they are so atmospheric and perfect. One such place was Schongau, which we visited the next day. Here, too, there were almost intact city walls to walk around. Birgit, who is from the more conventional North Germany, was completely blown away by the Bavarian locals, who do indeed walk around in all seriousness in Dirndls and Lederhosen. It was Father's Day, so we used that as an excuse to eat gigantic ice creams, which made us feel sick for the rest of the day.

A slight Sat Nav malfunction took us through the middle of Freiburg, rather than round the edge. I'd visited the city once before, a few years previously, in order to see the band Richmond Fontaine in a truly ghastly spit and sawdust pub called Café Atlantik. Suddenly, we found ourselves driving right past the front of this doubtful venue (where smoking is still allowed). The "rider" for the band back then consisted of thirty-six bottles of a rather pleasant Pilsner beer called Fucking Hell. In a clever scam, Hell is the German word for light beer and Fucking is a village in Austria. In fact, it's brewed at the *Waldhaus Brauerei* in the Black Forest and distributed from Berlin, so has absolutely nothing to do with Fucking. After an initial ban on the grounds of decency, the PR job was complete and it's now a common sight in bars across Germany.

The afternoon found us gliding along the side of the Bodensee (Lake Constance) where Austria, Switzerland and Germany meet. We were on the German side and chanced upon an incredible lakeside town called Meersburg, where we climbed the precipitous streets and marvelled at the Zeppelin buzzing overhead, carrying sightseers on a tour of the lake.

Somehow forever associated with people's idea of German engineering and innovation, a Zeppelin is a rigid airship named after Count Ferdinand von Zeppelin, who pioneered airship development in the early twentieth century in nearby

Friedrichshafen. Zeppelin's ideas were first developed in 1893, before the first flight in 1900.

Airships were seen as an attractive form of air travel in the early 20th century. They were also used as military aircraft, carrying out bombings in World War 1. In the 1930s, you could even (if you had the money) cross the Atlantic Ocean in a luxury airship. All that ended when the hydrogen-filled Hindenburg crashed in a fireball on May 6, 1937 in Lakehurst, New Jersey. The cause of the explosion is still unknown. Luckily, no one was killed, but the reputation of airships was destroyed.

The reason we could see a Zeppelin flying over Lake Constance is the Zeppelin NT (New Technology) project, started by the *Zeppelin Luftschifftechnik* company in Friedrichshafen in the late nineties. It used modern technology and design innovations to create a more manoeuvrable and efficient airship. The prototype NT 07 had its first 45-minute flight on September 18, 1997. So far, four Zeppelins have been built, and two are flying, one in Germany and the other in America.

UNLUCKY FOR SOME

When you are driving in Europe in a right-hand drive vehicle, you have to be extra alert. Overtaking is particularly difficult, and we hardly did any of it at all, except on motorways and dual carriageways. It's my duty to peer round whatever vehicle we are following and try to work out whether it's safe to pass it. As my sense of spatial awareness is terrible and my driving experience very limited, it is almost impossible for me to make such judgements. This resulted, particularly on the little roads of Sicily, in many miles being spent behind slow, wheezing tractors, rather than risk a collision.

Birgit, as we know, is an expert driver, but you can't see out of the back of Polly and the mirrors are unreliable. This is especially true at any junction or roundabout, where it is crucial to be able to see what traffic is approaching from the left. Sitting on the left, it is my job to look carefully and report to the driver whether it is safe to pull out. So far, it had not gone too badly. If anything, we always erred on the side of caution, because, even with a clear view, it's hard for me to judge relative speeds of approaching vehicles. Our luck was to run out shortly after leaving Meersburg.

I now realise that what we should have done was established a clear routine for junctions. What was actually happening was that Birgit would ask a question and I would answer it. For example,

"Is it safe for me to pull out?" - Yes / No.

"Is there anything coming?" - Yes / No.

As you can see, if the question is misunderstood, the wrong answer is given. In this particular case, we stopped at a junction on a small road on the outskirts of a town called Tengen. In the distance, coming from the left, I could see a car, so in my opinion, it wasn't safe to pull out. The problem was that I misheard Birgit's question. Whereas I thought she had asked if there was anything coming, she had, in fact, asked if the road was free. My answer was "Yes", i.e. there was something coming. Thinking that "Yes" meant the road was free, Birgit pressed the accelerator and started to pull out.

"No, no, stop!" I shouted, and of course, Birgit slammed

on the brakes. Immediately, there was a sickening crunch behind us. It was startlingly loud and the impact was forceful enough to push us a metre or so forwards. It was clear that whoever was behind us had smashed straight into the back of Polly.

After a moment or two of stunned silence, I opened the door and stepped out, expecting to see a scene of devastation. For all I knew, the driver behind could have been injured, and I expected at the very least that we would have major dents and that all the lights would be smashed and unusable. This would mean we wouldn't be able to continue our journey. As I walked round, the gentleman driving the other car also emerged, looking slightly ashen-faced, and immediately apologised. This reminded me straight away that, as far as I knew, anybody crashing into the back of somebody else is automatically responsible for the accident. This made me feel immediately better, and this sense of relief increased on noting that there didn't appear to be a single mark on his car.

Plucking up courage to turn around, I could see that the back of Polly was undented, and that the only sign that anything had happened was a minor scratch on the paintwork, which I thought I could probably easily patch up myself. It appeared that we had got away with it. The Swiss driver of the other vehicle remained apologetic, but we agreed that there seemed to be almost no damage.

What I should have done, of course, was take photographs, exchange full insurance details, etc, but in the end I merely accepted the business card he offered me and we parted. At one stage, I had to give Birgit a small kick, because she was starting to explain why we had started to pull out and then stopped. I feared this could be interpreted as admitting some kind of guilt, but in principle I knew that legally, the other guy was responsible.

The mood was very downbeat as we progressed towards that evening's campsite, because in my heart, I knew that, legalities aside, I had been responsible for the accident. Things didn't improve as we arrived at the campsite. We had chosen it because it advertised an indoor pool, but in actual fact it was effectively a holiday camp for children and, unbeknownst to us, it was the half-term holiday in Germany. Remember all that tiny print in the ACSI book? Yes, we had let ourselves down by not studying it quite closely enough. Just for this week, it was technically high season, so the price had more than doubled from the twenty euros we thought we were going to spend, to an astronomical forty-two euros. This was for a site where we wouldn't be able to use any of the facilities, due to their being completely full of children. They were all having, of course, a wonderful time, and good luck to them.

Things got worse when we opened the back door of the van. Inside, we discovered that the impact had caused all sorts of damage to the door and some internal fittings. Why hadn't we looked earlier? We must have been mad, but the fact was that we'd just been in a state of shock and not thinking straight. It was clear that this was going to be an insurance job, and not nearly as minor as we had thought.

Feeling now, frankly, that we just wanted to get home, we bedded down for the night and awoke to the news, via a text on my phone, that one of my closest and most loved friends had died overnight. Peter had been ill for a long time, so it wasn't totally unexpected, but nonetheless it was a terribly sad day that put our minor woes into stark perspective.

Life had to go on, and where better for it to continue than the beautiful Black Forest? The Sat Nav, for a change, did its job and took us through all sorts of lovely areas that we never would have found by simply taking major roads from town to town. For a lunch picnic, we ended up in one of the most idyllic spots imaginable, at the top of a steep hill called the *Kaiserstuhl* (Emperor's Chair), not far from Freiburg. Allegedly, the vineyards we could see stretching away for miles into the distance originated from plants brought across the Mediterranean from Mesopotamia in Roman times.

The hills are volcanic in origin, and the wine is blessed by Germany's sunniest climate. We sat at a picnic table with a view of the perfectly presented vineyards, and not a car, lorry, bicycle or tractor to be seen. Ah, Germany, so neat, tidy and serene.

Soon, we found ourselves crossing the Rhine into France, and chose to take some massively long toll tunnels through the Vosges. The campsite we stayed on was on the banks of the Moselle, in a little village could Liverdun. As we travelled through France, we noticed that many of the small towns and villages were absolutely deserted, with no sign of any pedestrians or shoppers anywhere. Liverdun was no exception, and we set out on a mission in search of somewhere to eat. It was not to be, but we found a huge abandoned secondary school that was for sale at the price of a one-bedroom flat where we come from. As well as being a centre for the manufacture of those delicious little cakes called *Madeleines*, Liverdun actually possessed a *château* which, with characteristic inevitability, was closed to the public, but did present a photo opportunity as I hammered forlornly on its firmly-barred doors.

On and on we travelled, driving through the picture postcard villages of Lorraine and past the poignant battlefields of Verdun. Ever since the beginning of our odyssey in Troyes we had been yearning for another *galette*, and had set our sights on finding one for lunch. We stopped to carry out this mission in Châlons en Champagne, a town with a fine cathedral and an atmosphere that was similar to Troyes but not nearly as spectacular. Considering that Troyes had had a *crêperie* on every corner, it wasn't unreasonable to expect something similar here, but after walking around for an hour and consulting various locals, we discovered that there was no *galette* anywhere to be purchased.

The lovely villages gave way to the hideous outskirts of Reims. It seemed as if the Sat Nav had invented a new command for us to programme in: "Take us past the most desolate, tumbledown, abandoned factories you can find", but eventually we reached the campsite. It turned out to be another holiday park, full of "Eurocamping" Brits, refusing to even attempt to speak in French. Thankfully, at least the price was at normal ACSI rates. As usually happens when UK families take over a campsite in France, there was nobody of any other nationality to be seen. I wonder why?

Nonetheless, it turned out to have the best facilities of anywhere we had stayed and even had a quite good, if expensive, restaurant. Here, we attempted to give some kind of symmetry to the arc of our journey by indulging in some seafood, even though we were nowhere near the sea. I had a pot of *moules*, while Birgit had some unidentified white fish. She pointed out, correctly, that one of the main things she had been looking forward to on our journey was eating delicious fresh fish, but that we had not had a single opportunity to do so. On the campsite was a huge artificial lake, complete with a sandy beach. The water was delightfully warm, so we lolled in there for an hour or so.

As we were back in France, we obviously had croissants for breakfast, before setting out for the compulsory valedictory supermarket shop, to cram the van with wine, cheese and diesel. Everywhere we had been, along with the local supermarket brands, we had been tempted by various branches of Aldi and Lidl, where it is always fascinating to see how they cleverly tailor their offering to the country, or even the region, they are in. Wanting to remain pure in our allegiance to France, we opted for a good old Intermarché, where a perfectly good bottle of wine can be had for just over a euro.

Just outside Dieppe, we found a charming, unpretentious little seaside resort called Pourville Sur Mer. Despite its inauspicious nature, it had some interesting history. We wondered why there were several Canadian war memorials in the town and made some enquiries.

On August 19, 1942, Operation Jubilee was launched

on the beaches of the Dieppe area. The aim was to create a breach in the German defences and gain control of the port of Dieppe. The main memorial we saw honours the Canadian troops who lost their lives during the raid. The Canadians landing at Pourville had been initially able to gain some degree of surprise. The South Saskatchewan Regiment and Queen's Own Cameron Highlanders of Canada assaulted the beaches. At first, resistance was light, but opposition increased as they crossed the River Scie and headed for Dieppe. The enemy was able to fire intensely on the Canadians from dominant positions on the cliffs east of Pourville and from high ground to the west. Both regiments were forced to withdraw, and lost heavily as they did so. The raid failed to achieve its objectives. The Canadian troops suffered mass casualties, losing over nine hundred men in nine hours, and, although many were rescued by Allied landing craft, others were forced to surrender.

Along the seafront, we came across display boards showing beautiful paintings and seascapes by Claude Monet. Many of them were of the beach and cliffs around Pourville, often at sunset, and showed what the scenery would have been like in more peaceful days. Monet spent the winter of 1882 in Pourville and enjoyed the time spent there so much that he returned with his family the following summer.

"La plage à Pourville, soleil couchant" is one of the most famous paintings he created while there, and has a story attached to it that occurred long after his death.

The painting shows the beach and cliffs at Pourville, with much of the scene taken up by sea and sky. In September 2000, it was stolen from the Poznan National Museum in Poland. It was cut out of its frame and replaced with a cardboard copy. The painting, the only one by Monet on public display in Poland, was valued at more than a million dollars. The theft was discovered on 19 September, 2000. A man had been seen making sketches of paintings in the museum two days before, but a police search for him was fruitless. Ten years later, *"La plage à Pourville"* was recovered in the southern Polish city of Olkusz. It was in the possession of a 41 year-old man, who was finally brought to justice, while the painting was returned to Poznan.

As we traversed the river marshes on a boardwalk, we came upon the exact spot where Monet had sat to create one of his better-known paintings, called *"Vallée de la Scie"* (1882). A display board was set up so that you could compare the painting with the reality. Very little seemed to have changed in the interim, but it was sobering to think of those Canadian troops, trapped there in 1942 with no escape.

As for dinner, well, would you believe it, the tiny little

campsite café offered a range of *galettes*. Ignoring the fact that the vinegary wine came from a box and that the *galettes* were pre-prepared ones brought from a supermarket, we tucked in as it's only possible to do on the last night of a holiday.

Back in England, where we were greeted by hideous traffic jams and - guess what - torrential rain, we arrived home, tired but satisfied with our efforts. Less satisfactory was what greeted us at our house. The one thing that I had been really missing was having a bath. Six weeks without one of those is serious deprivation in my mind, and the sense of anticipation as I walked up the path was intense. It turned out that the boiler had broken down and there was no hot water to be had.

"Oh well, at least we can have a decent cup of tea," I said, switching on the electric kettle. As it failed to make the expected hissing sound that kettles make, I gradually became aware that the entire house had fused and that no electricity was functioning. This led to a frantic rush to the deep freeze, where we discovered that everything had melted and had to be thrown away.

"Never mind, we could always sleep in the van," I suggested.

Birgit's frown told me all I needed to know.

Also by Oliver Gray:

VOLUME
A cautionary tale of rock and roll obsession

V.A.C.A.T.I.O.N.
Cautionary tales of travelling without style

ALAB (with Eddie Hardin)
35 years of musical mayhem on the road with the Spencer Davis Group

ACCESS ONE STEP
The official history of the Joiner's Arms

ZANDER
An Americana whodunnit

BANJO ON MY KNEE
A musical journey through the American south

All published by Sarsen Press, Winchester, UK